Adult Coloring Book
Relaxation

I0485648

Vol. 1

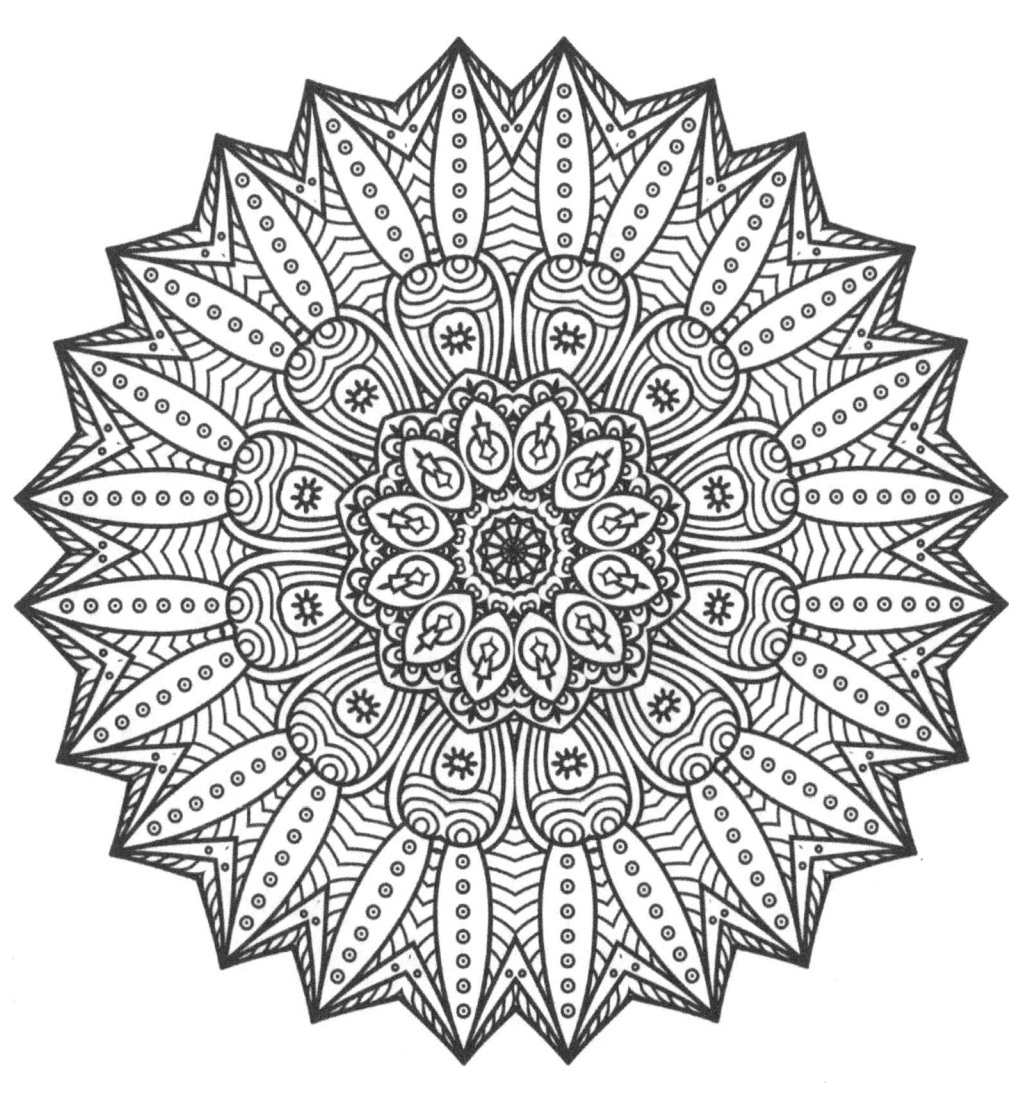

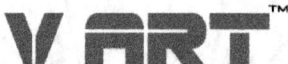

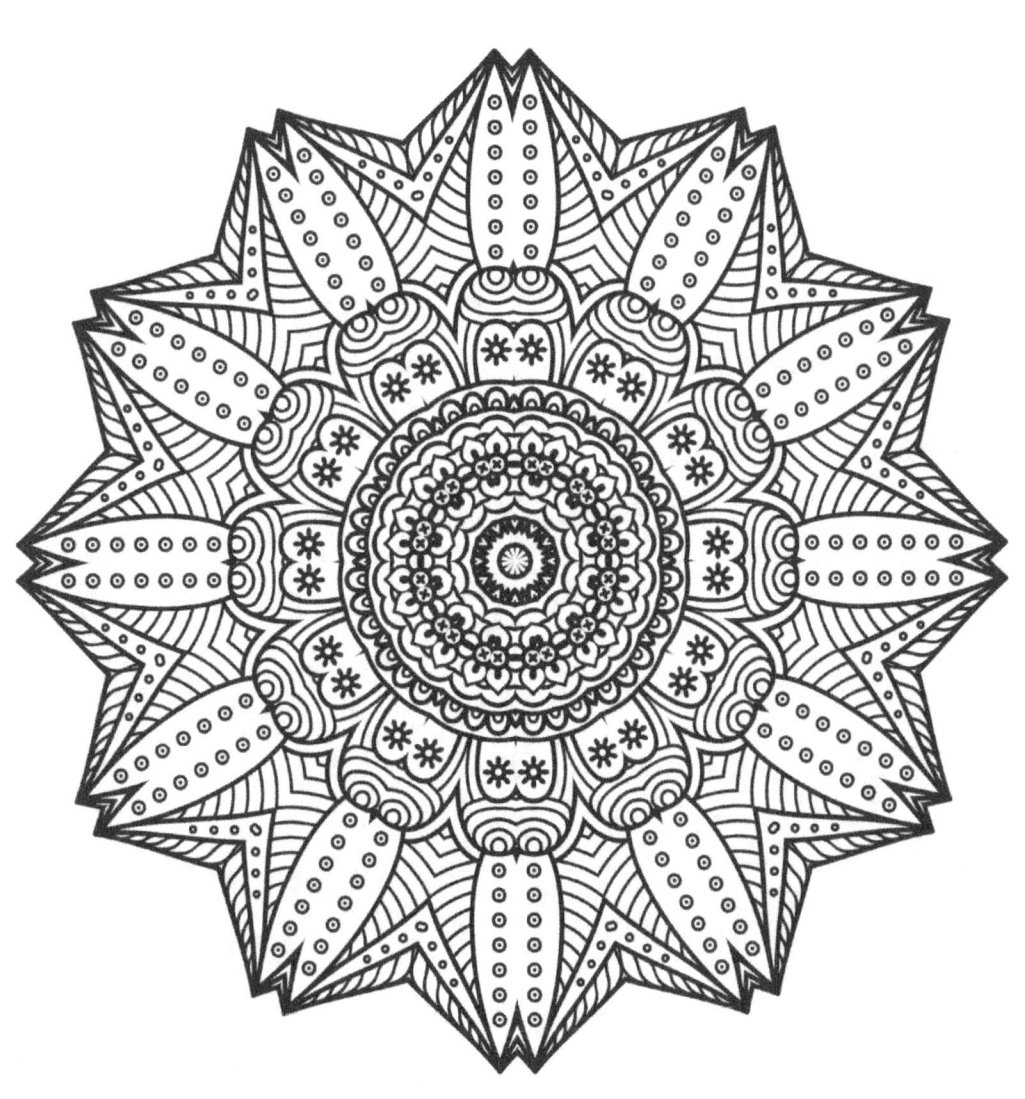

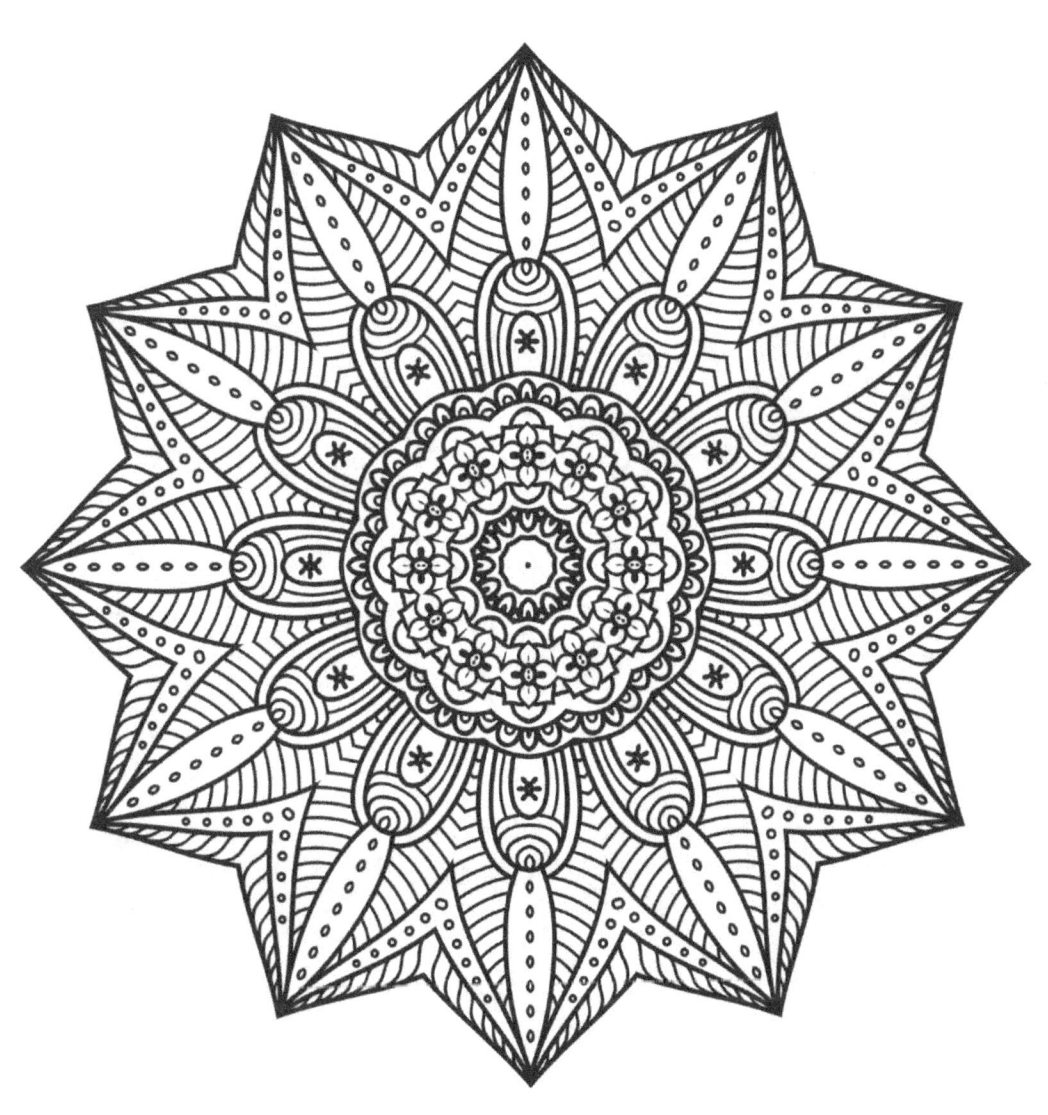

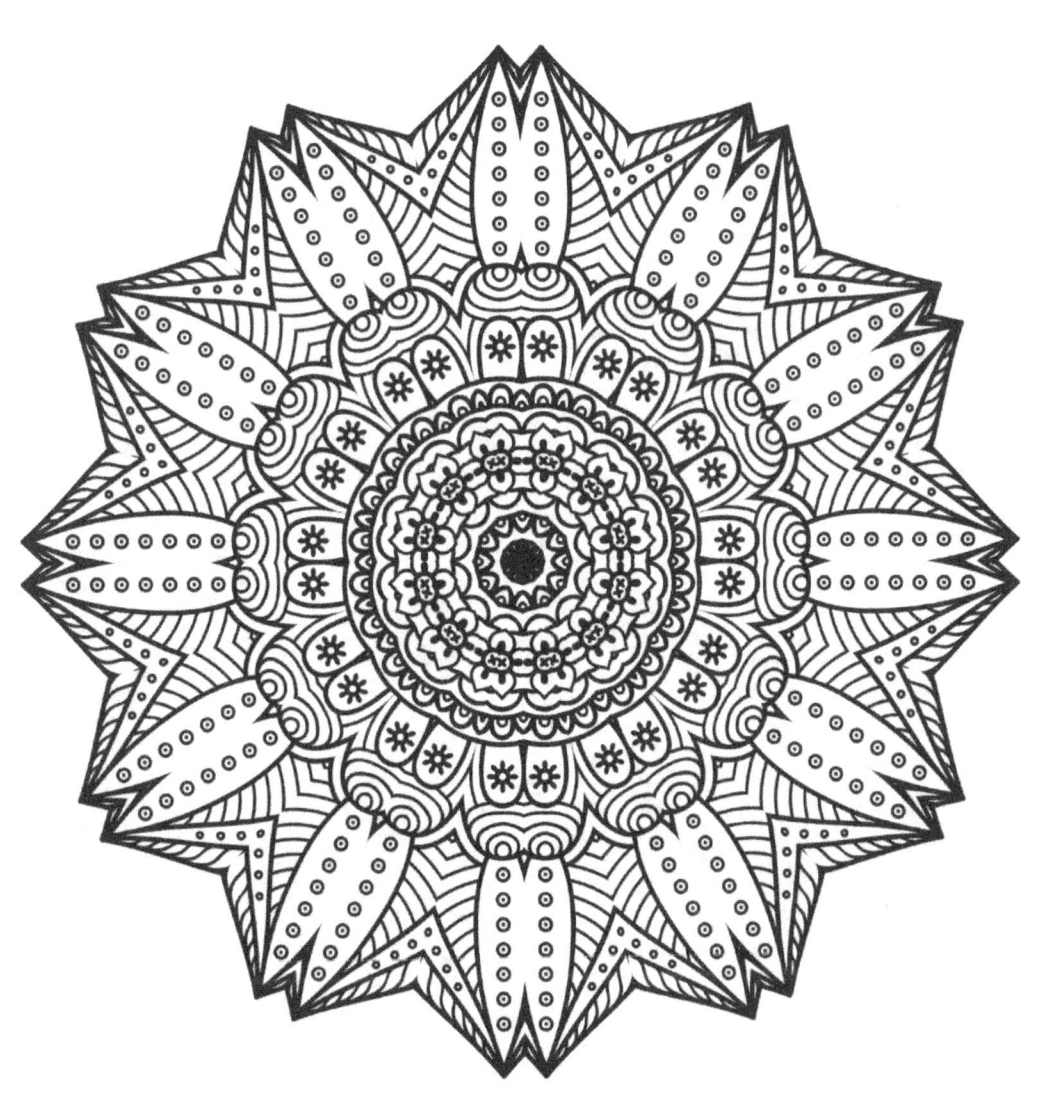

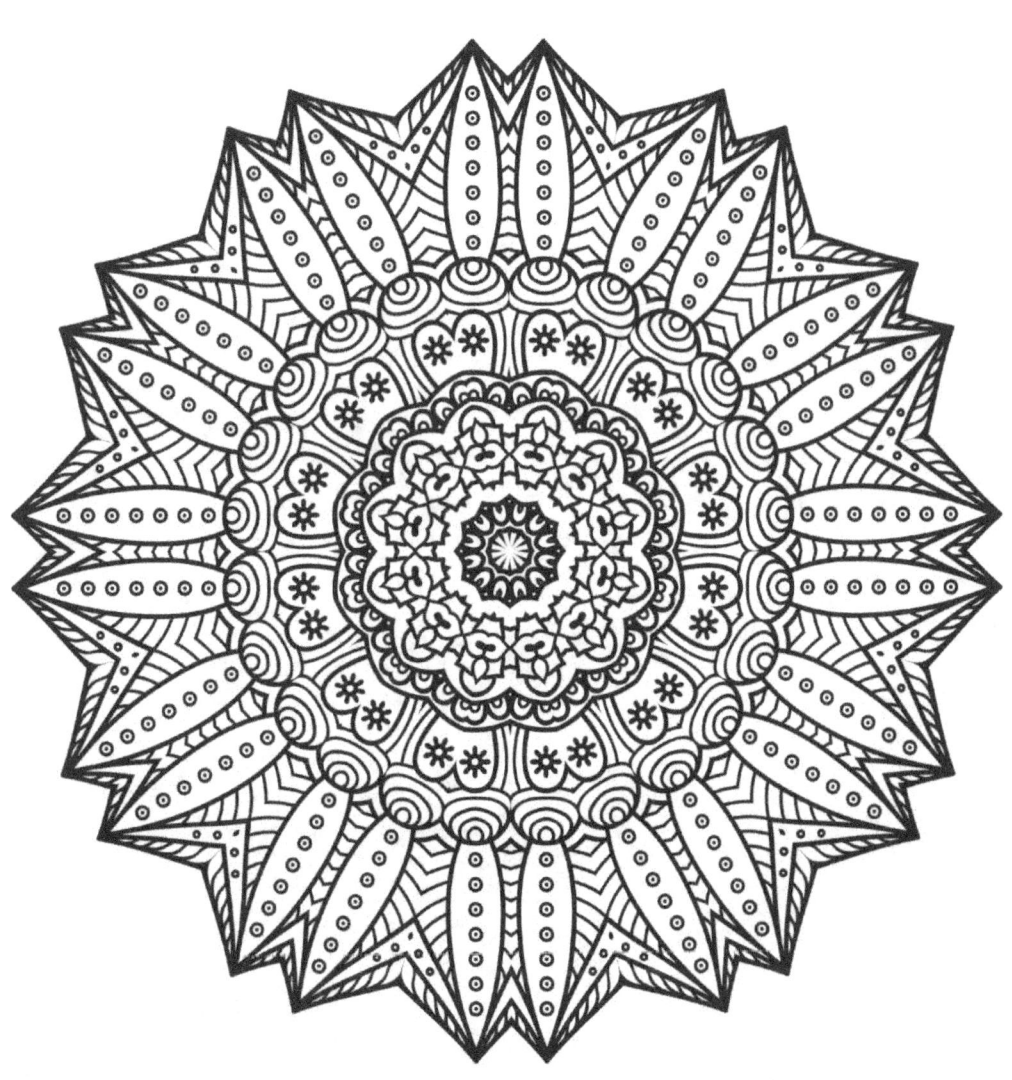

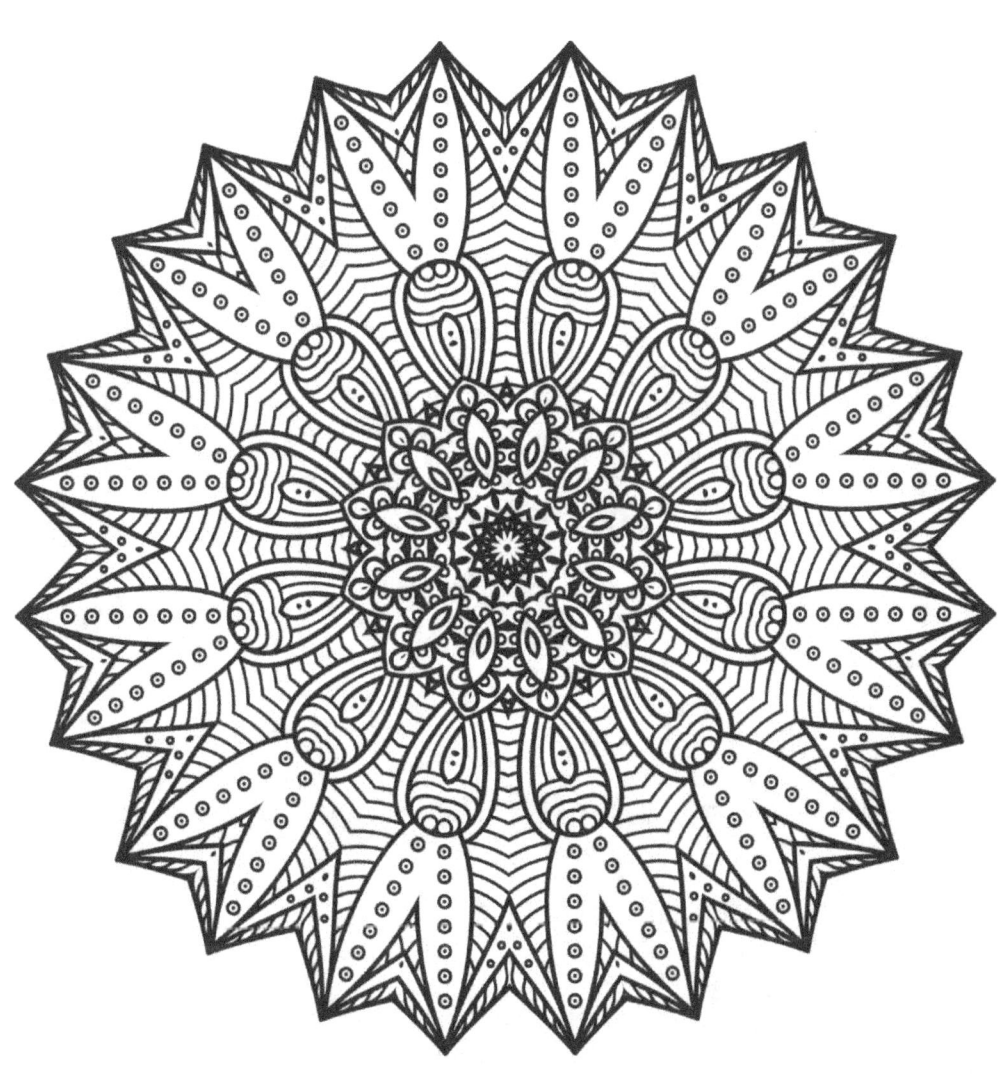

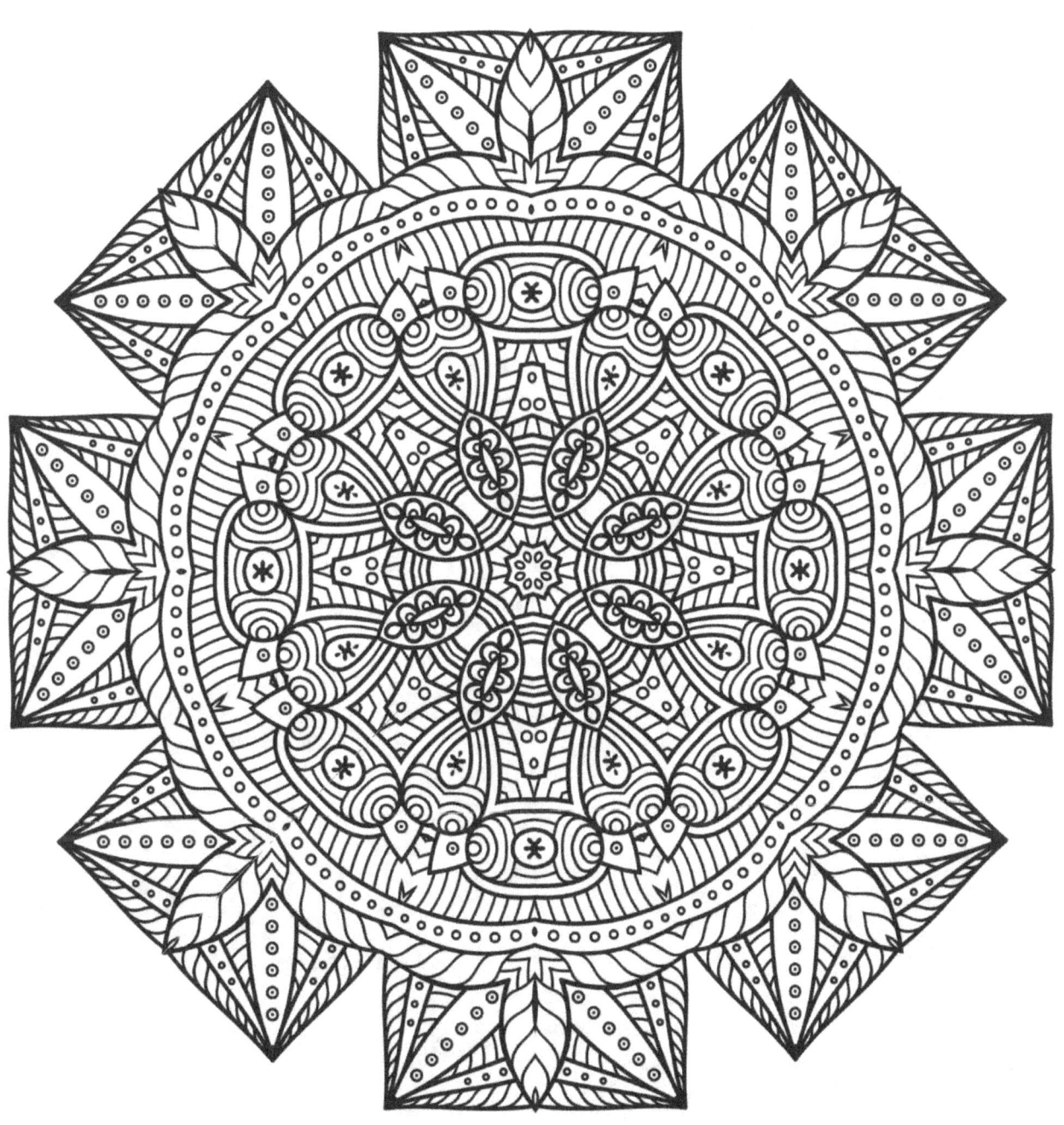

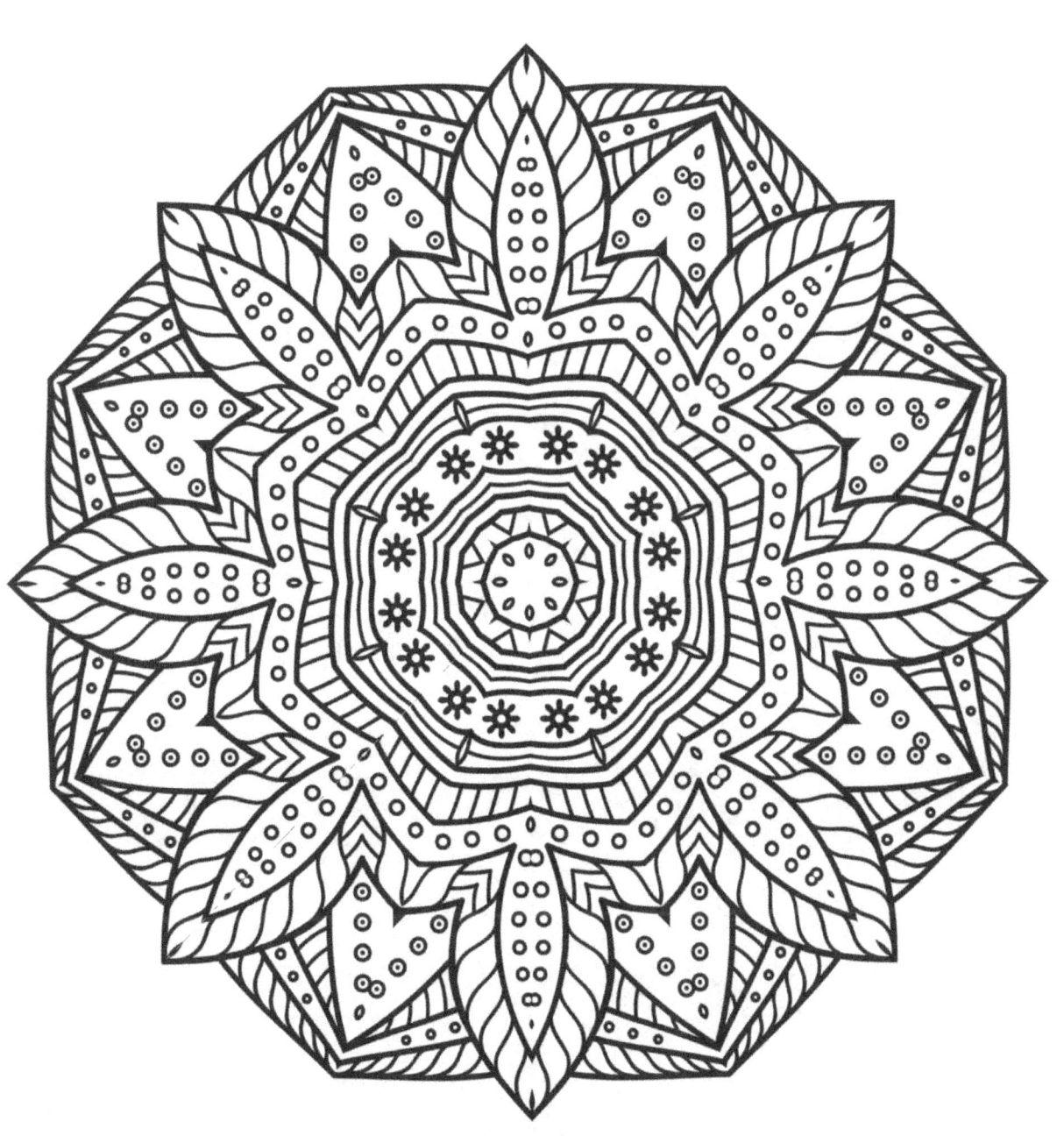

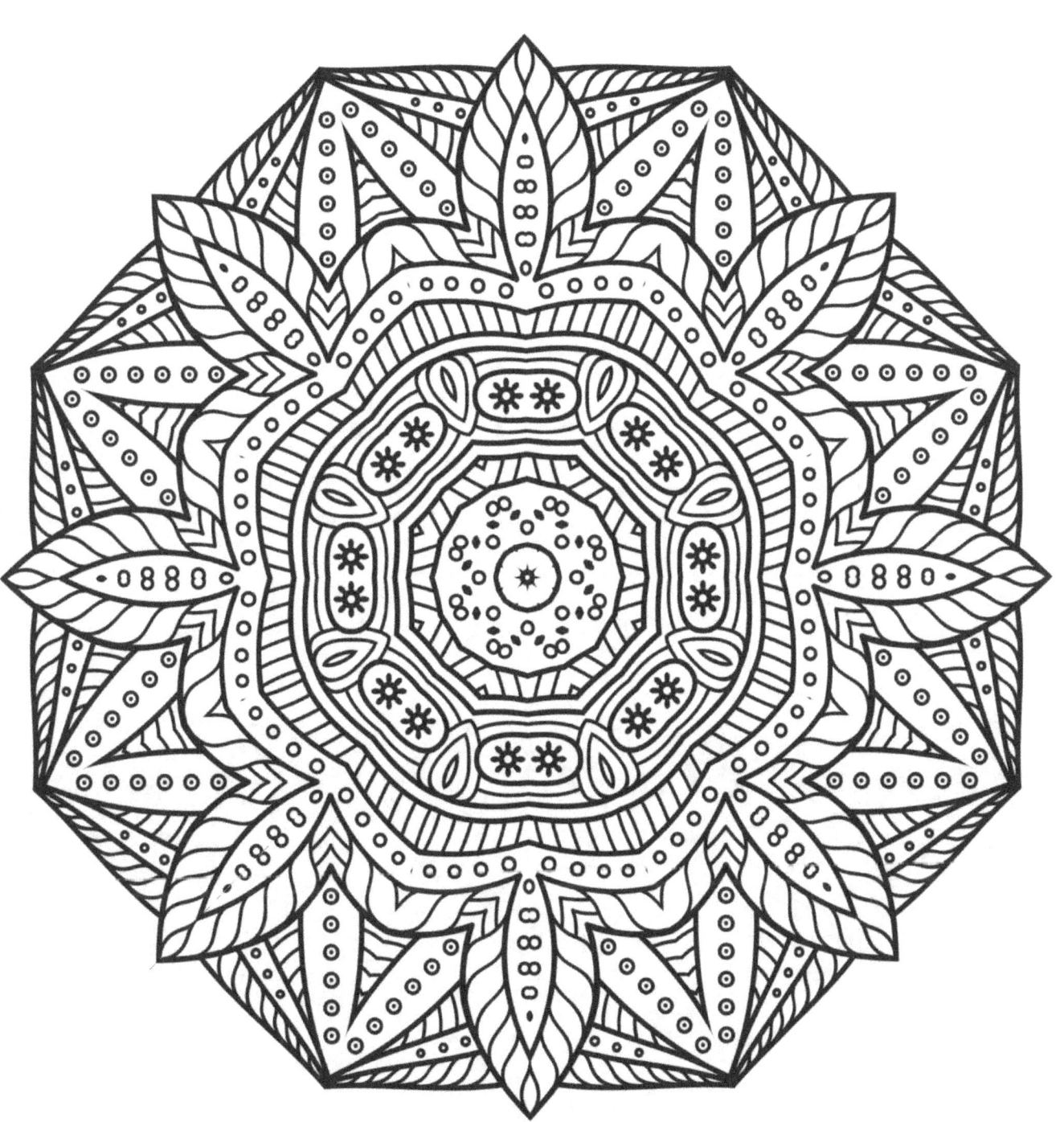

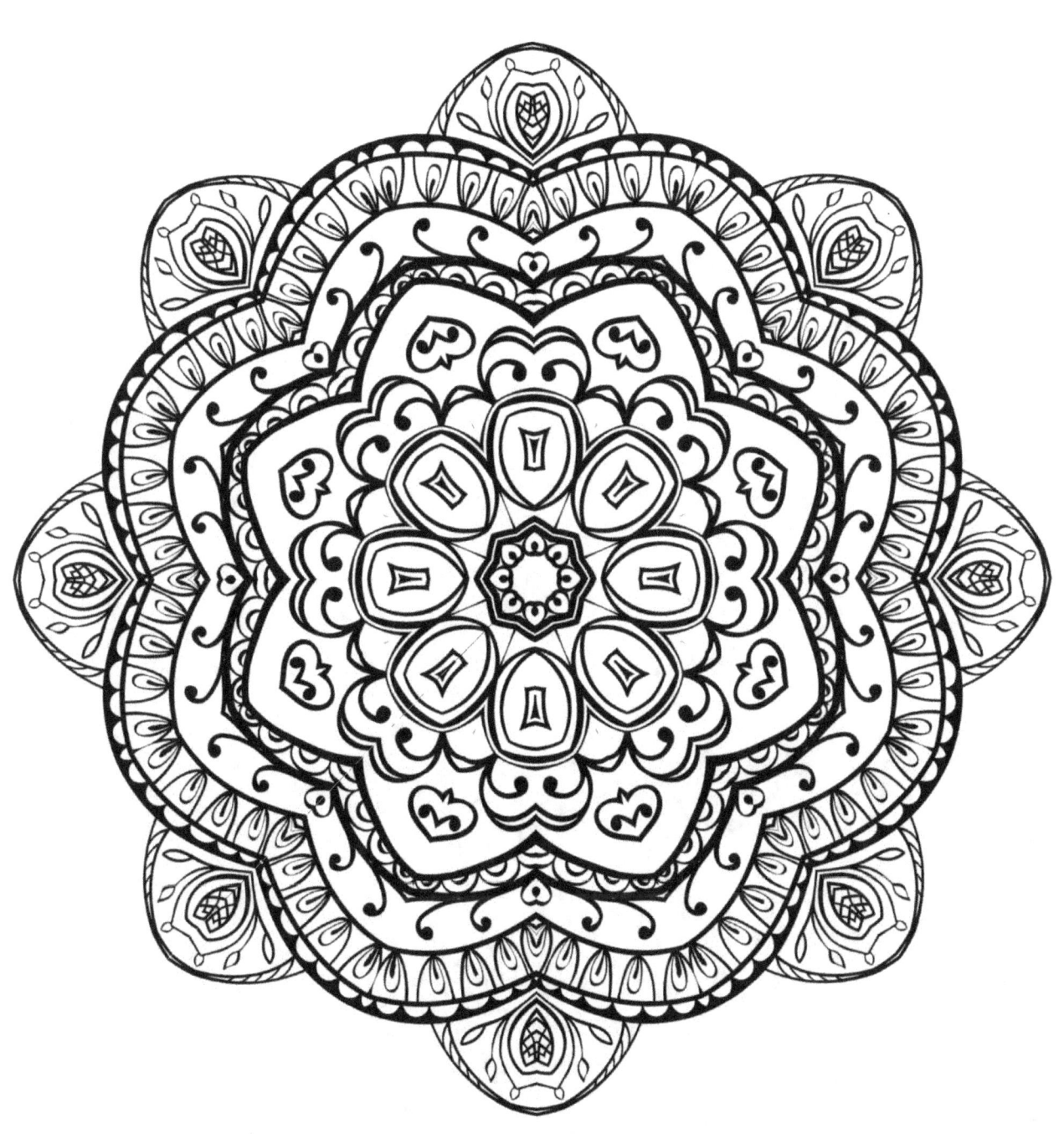

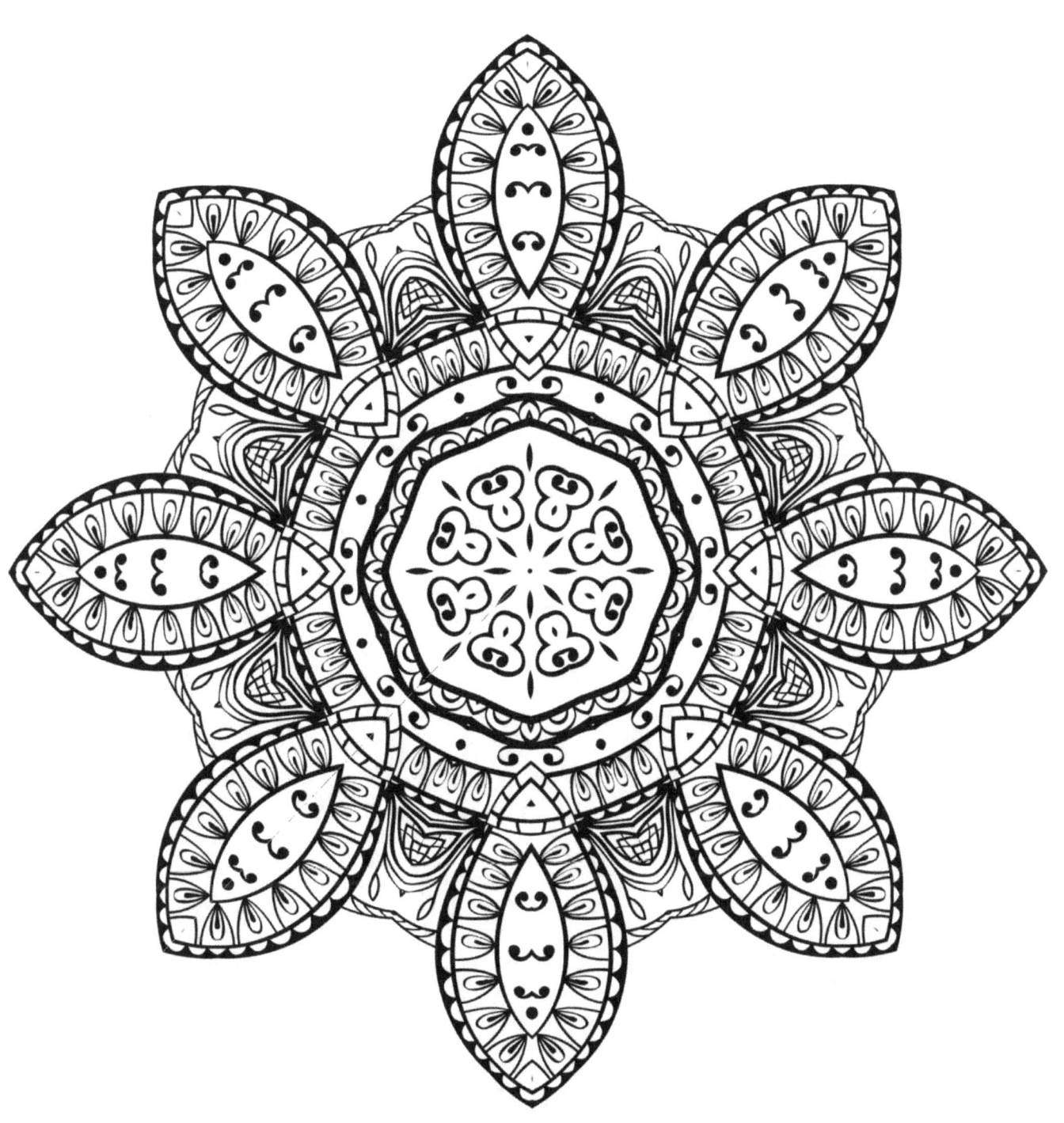

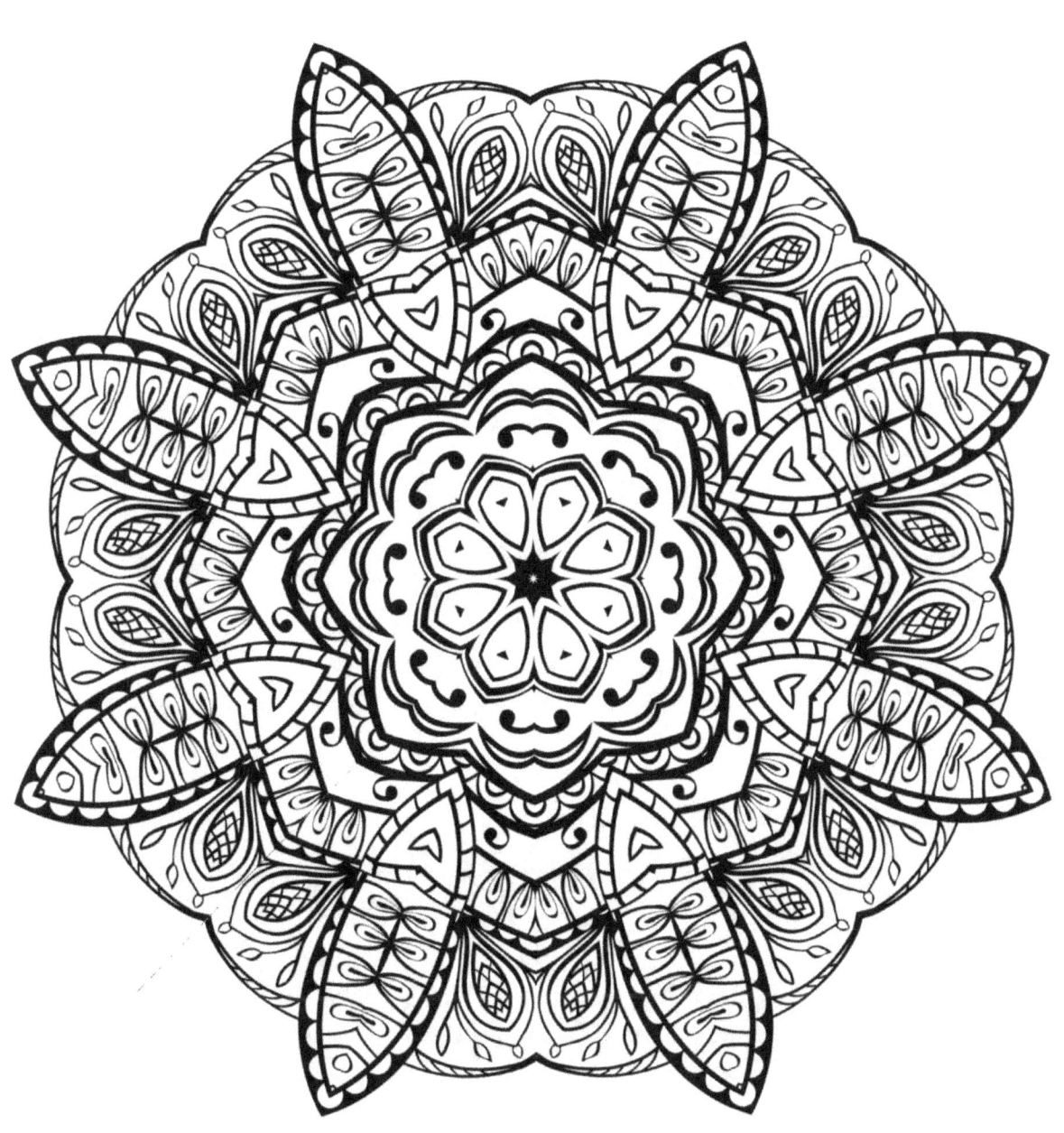

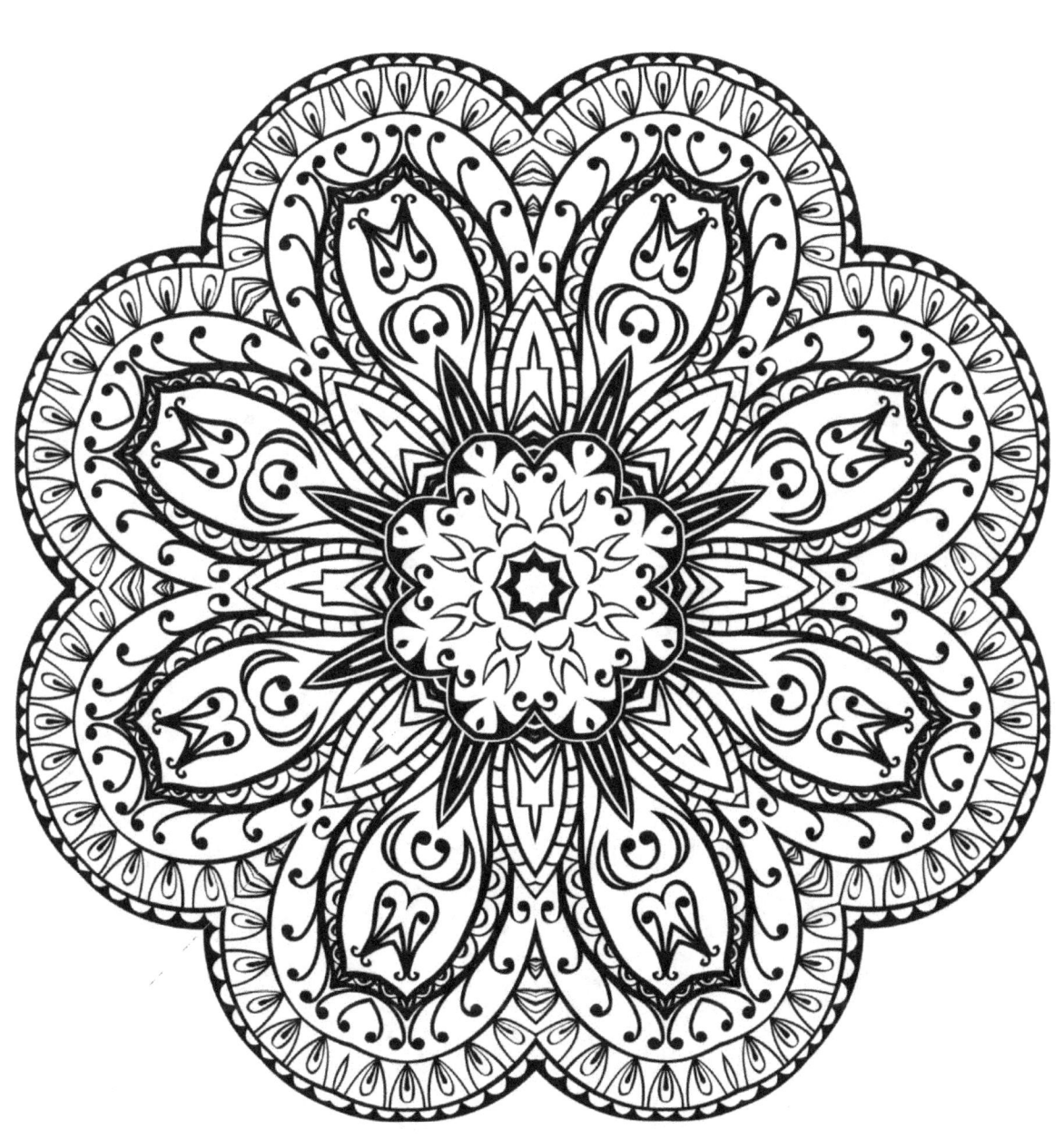

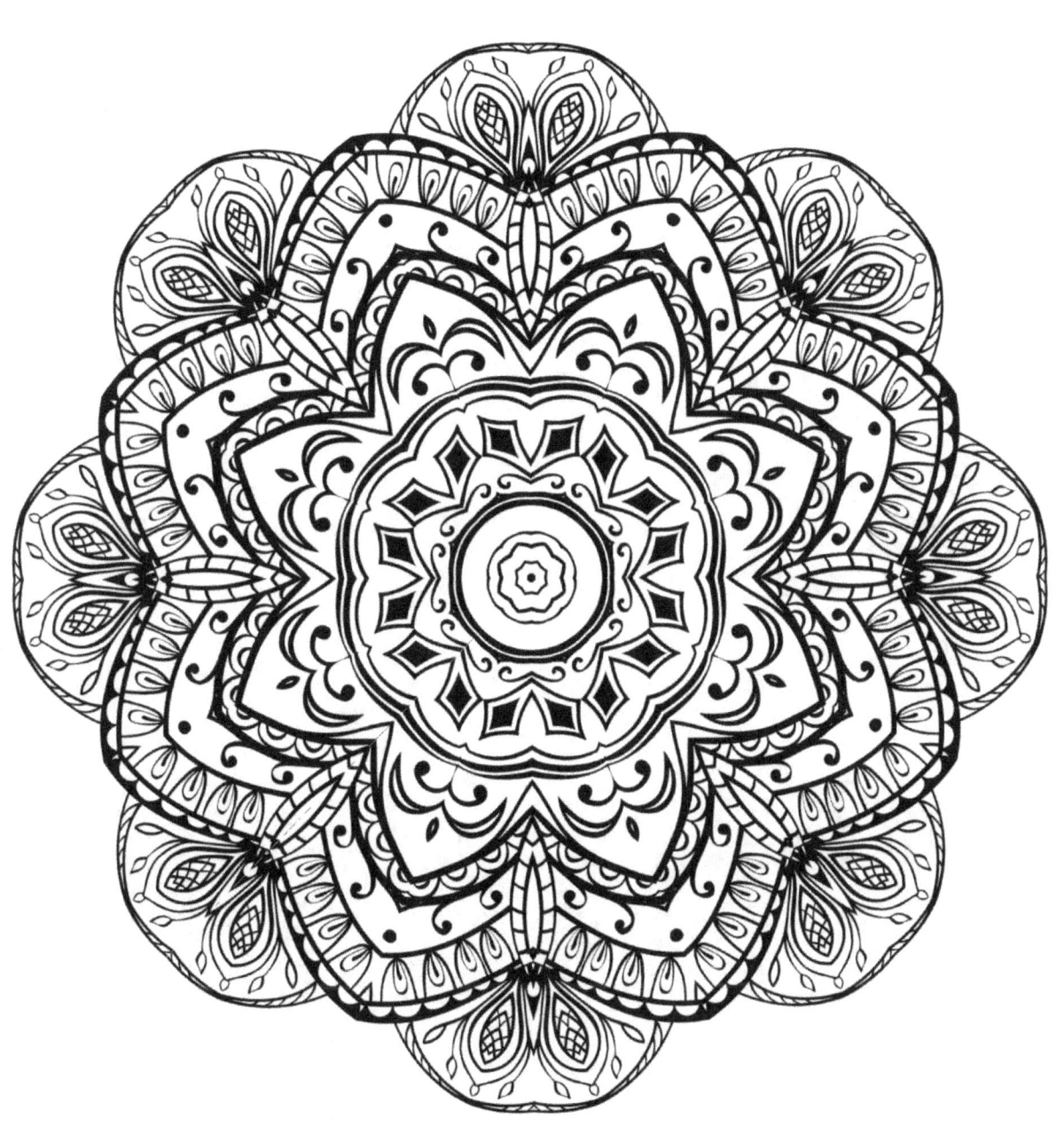

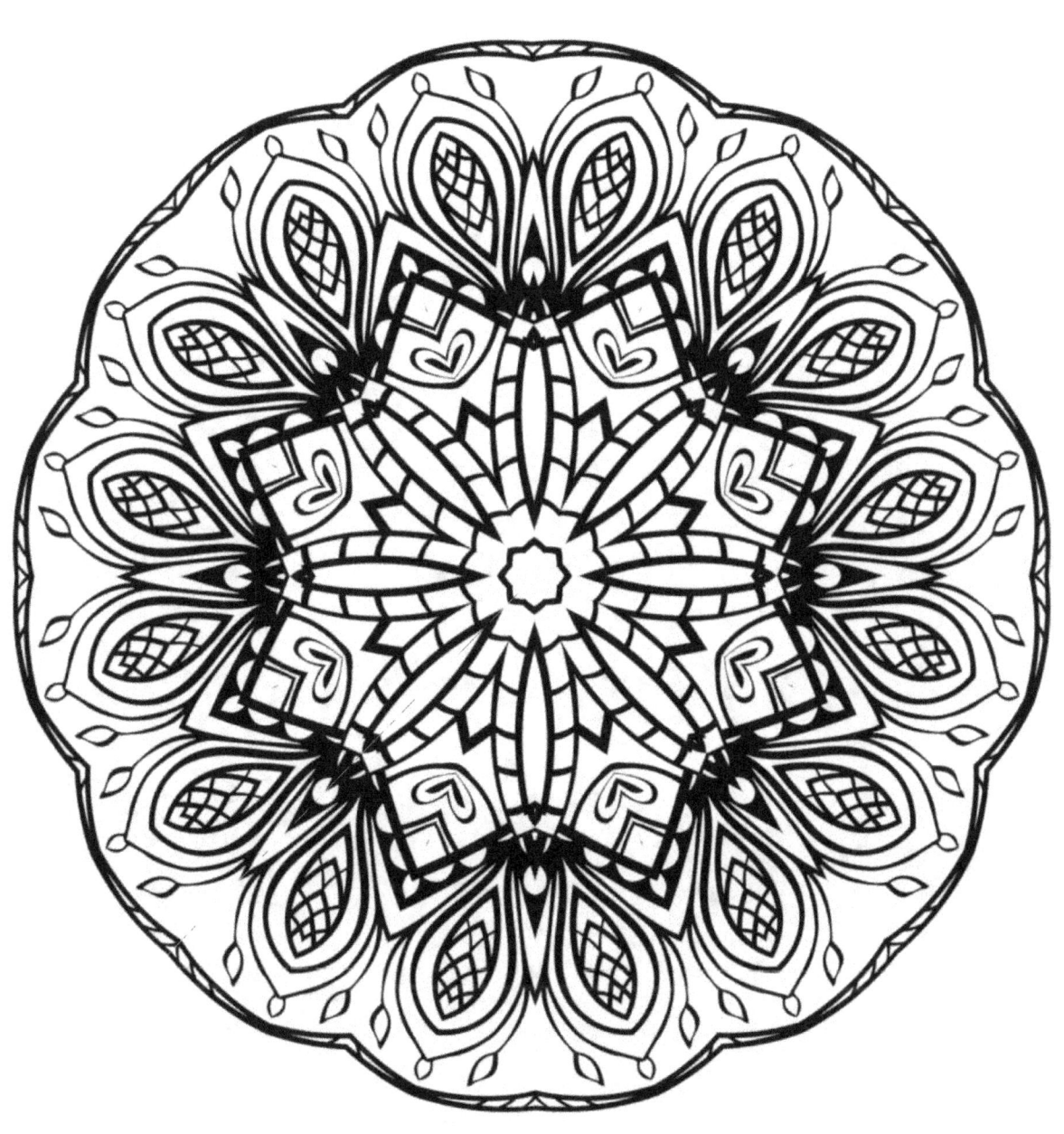

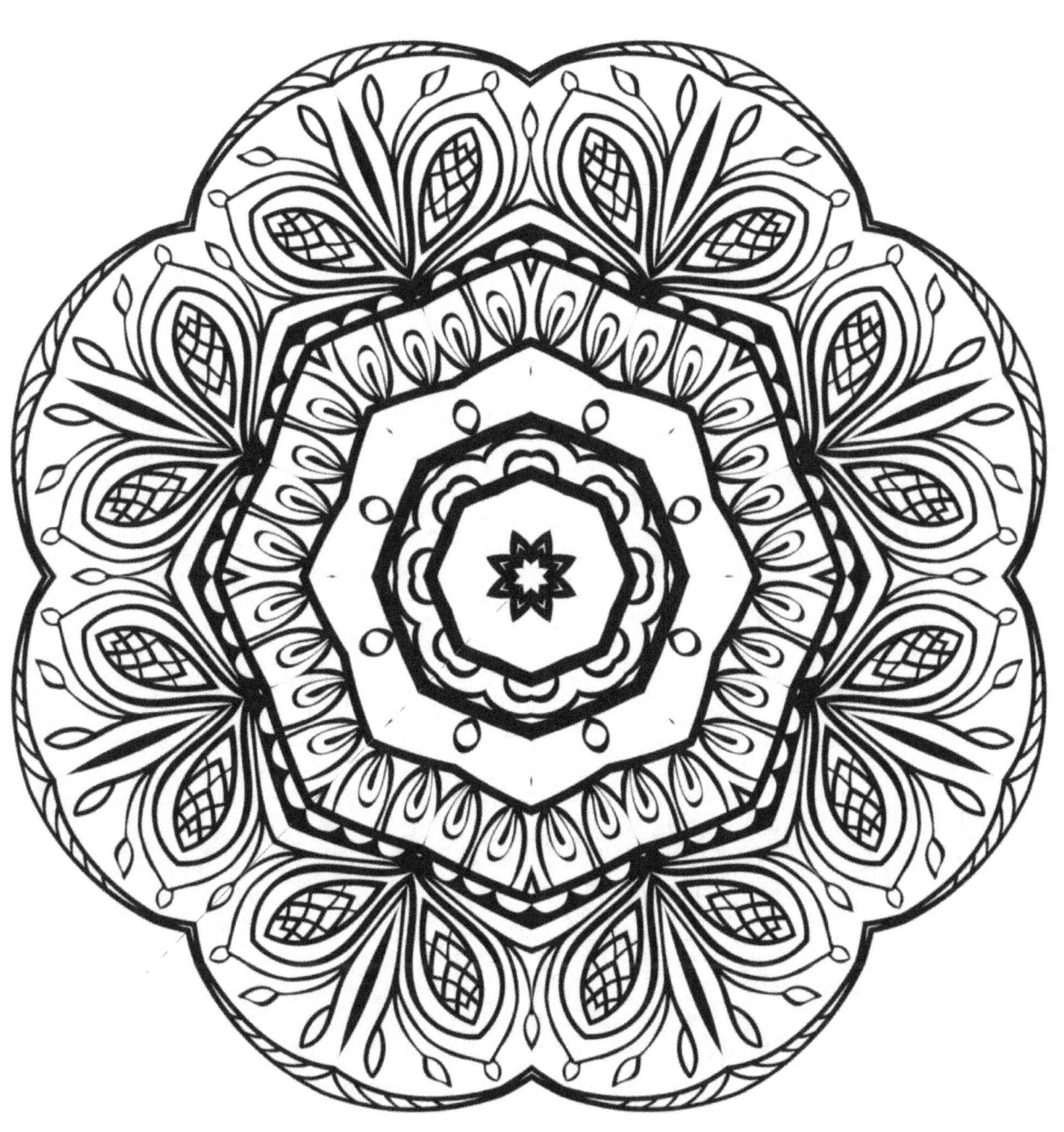

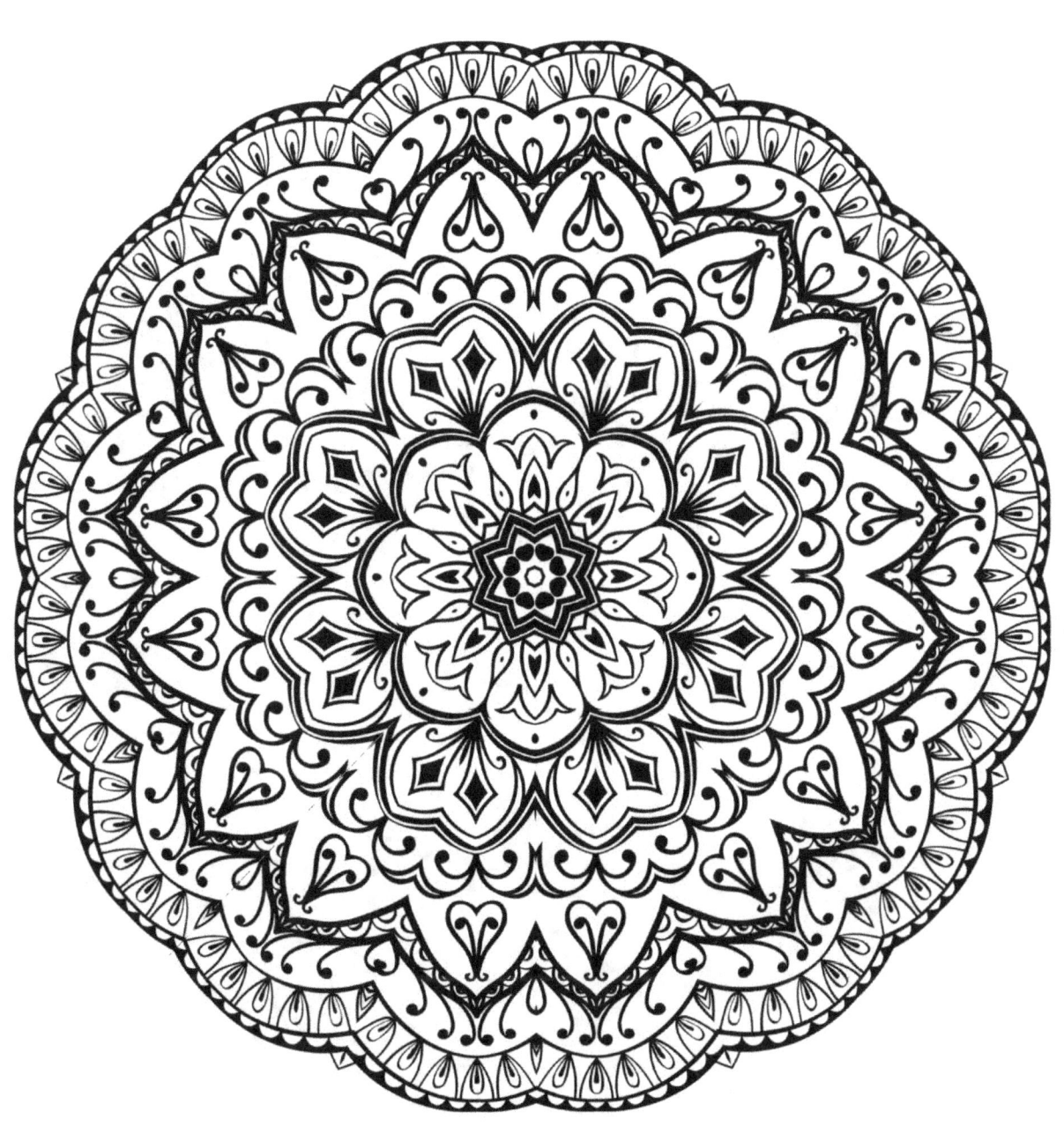

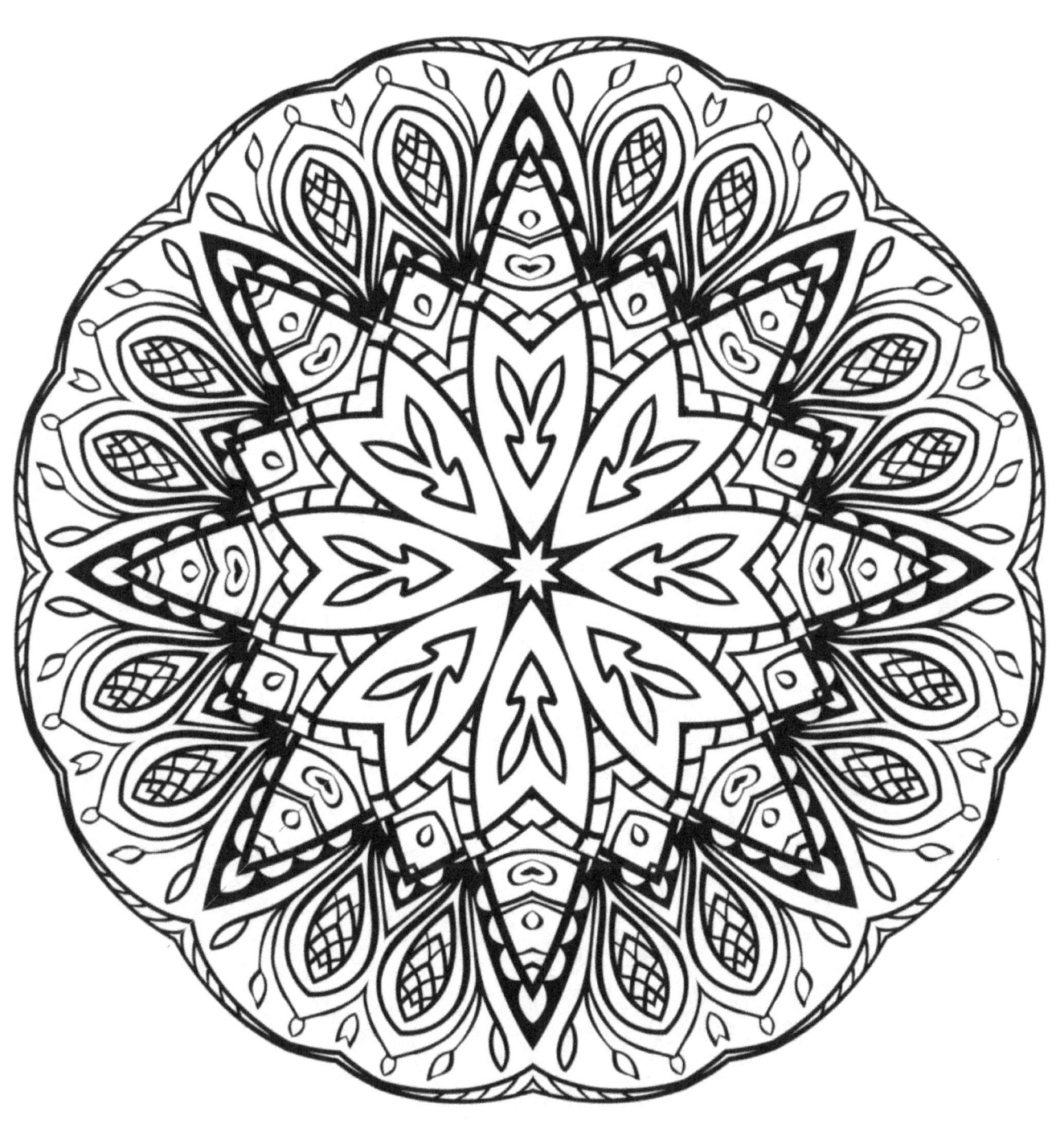

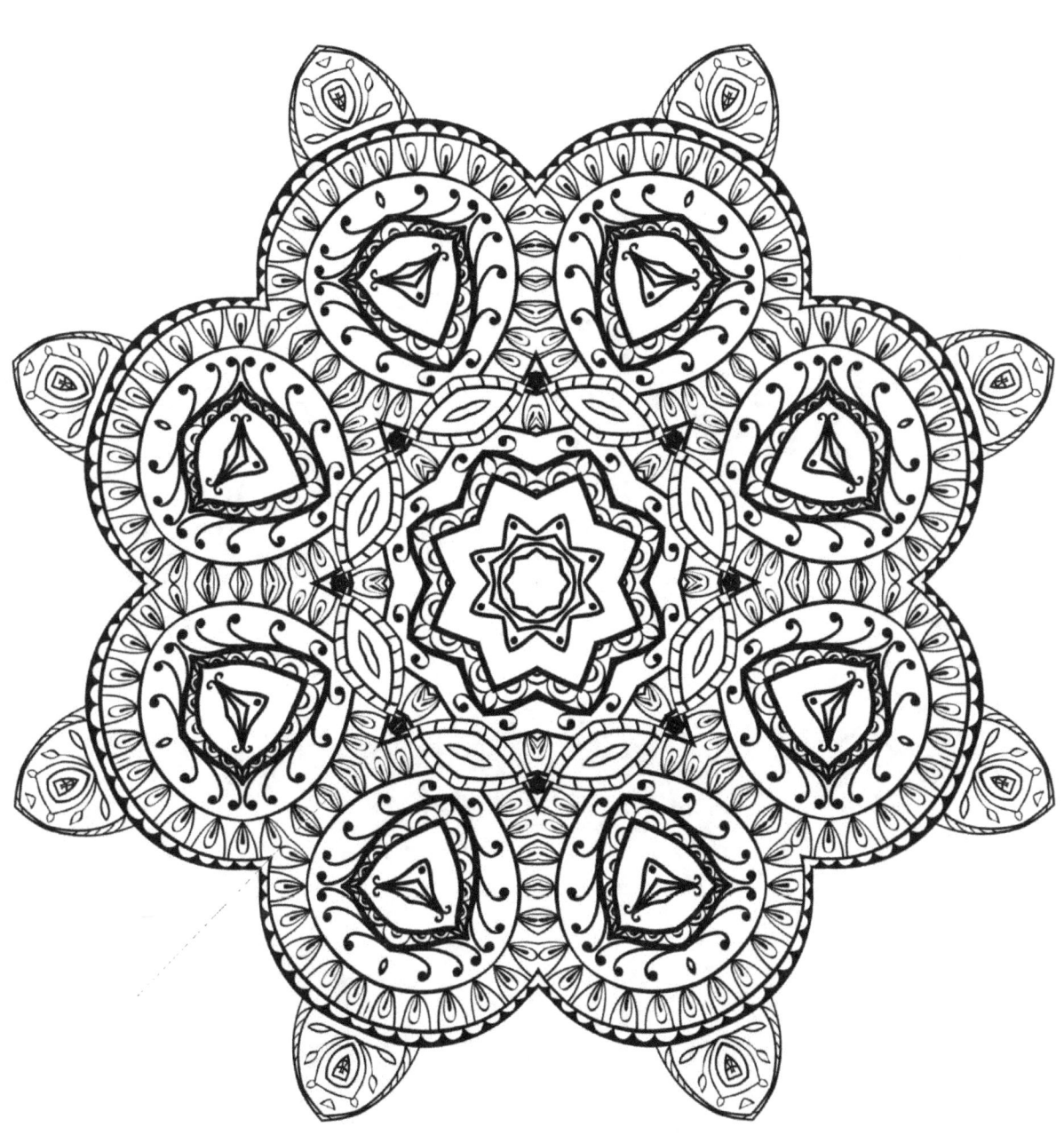

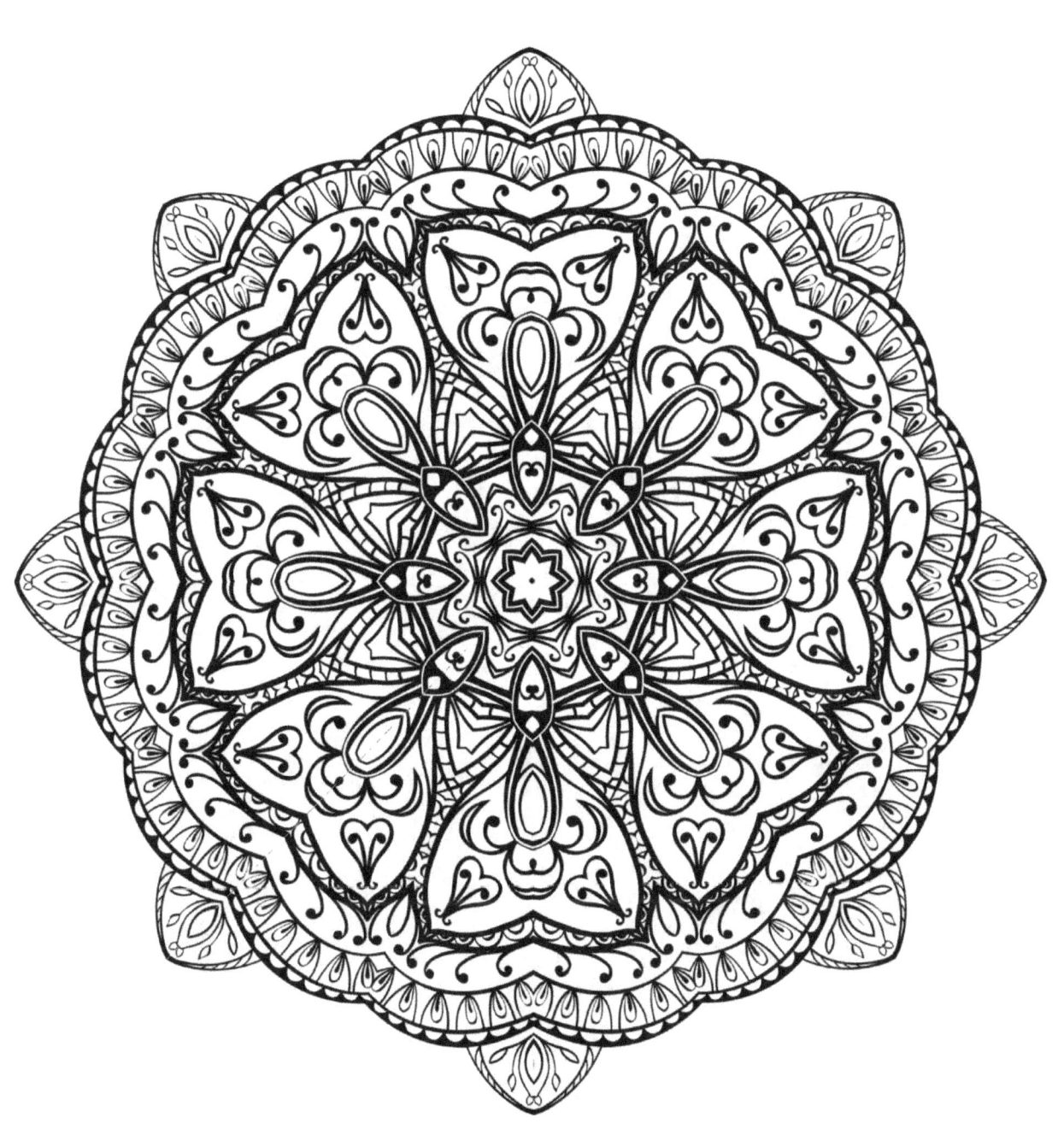

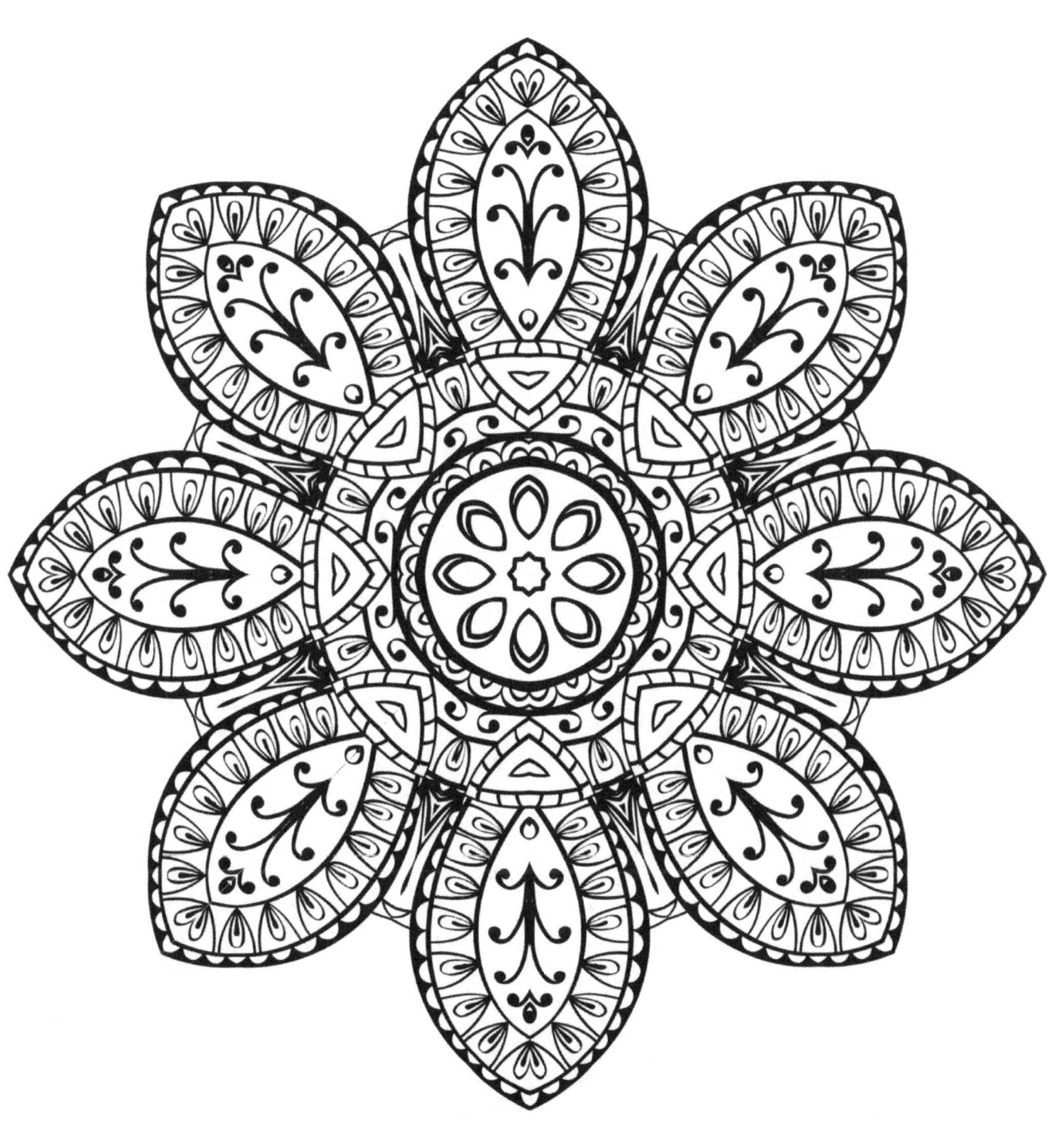

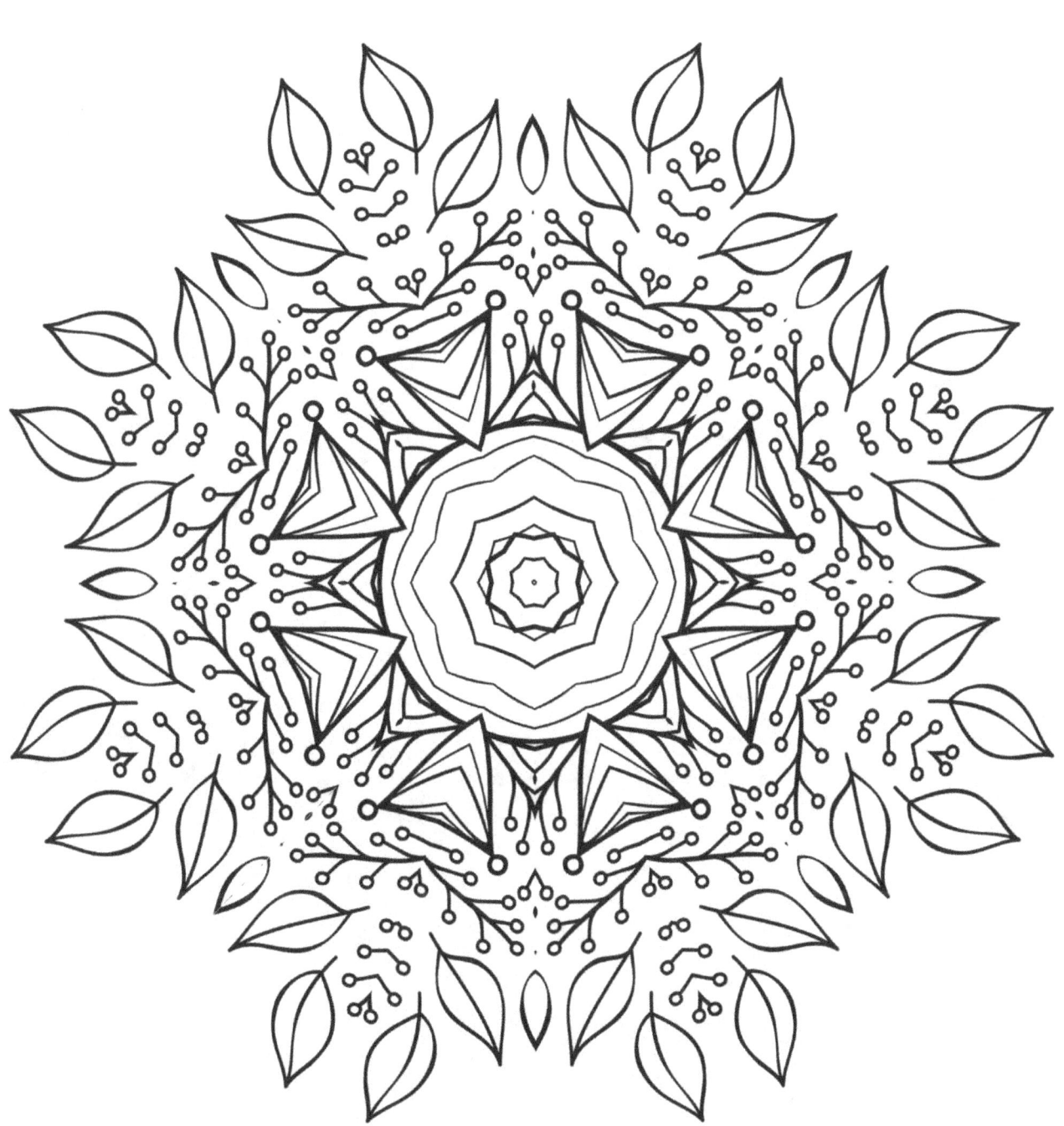

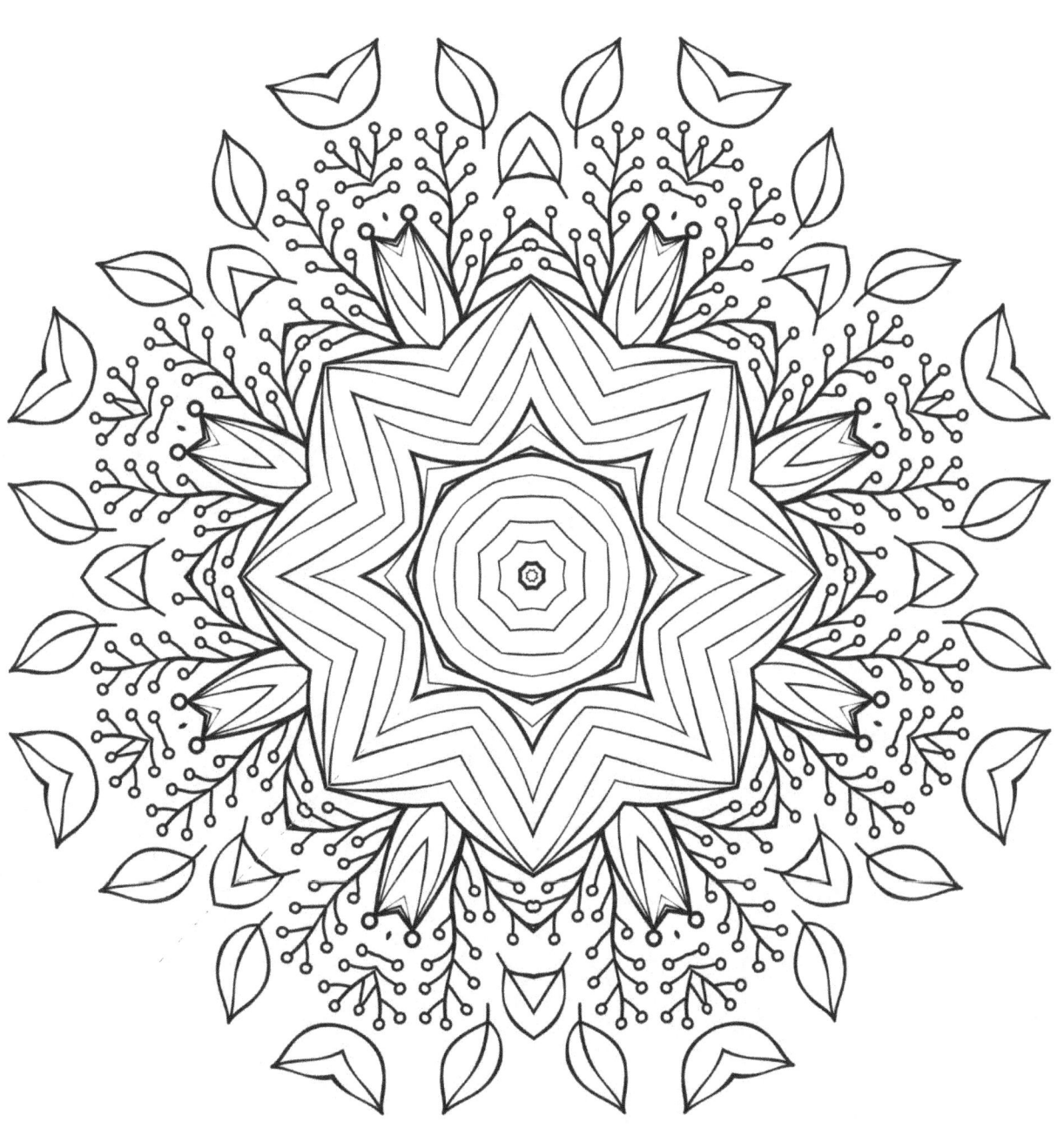

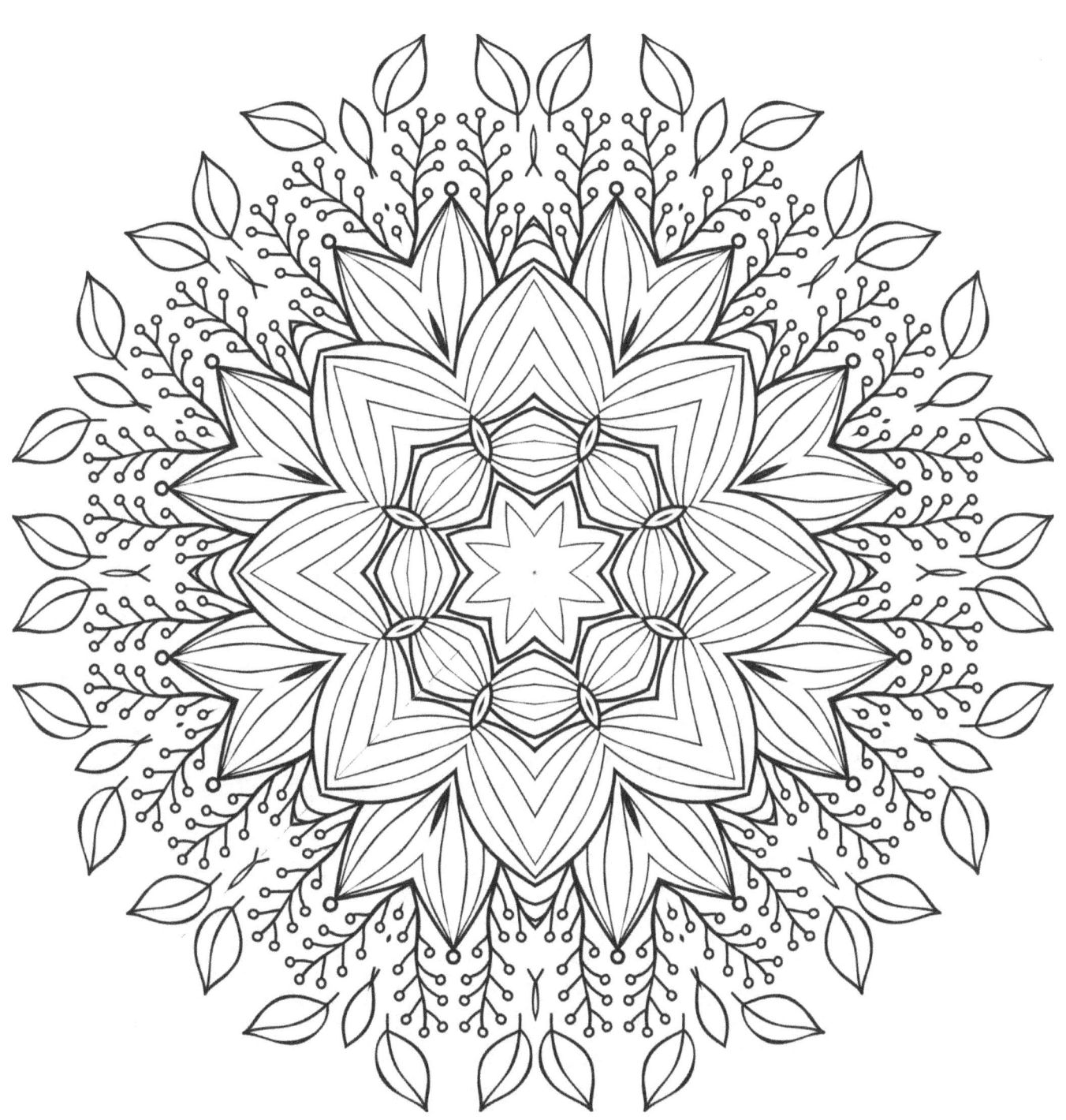

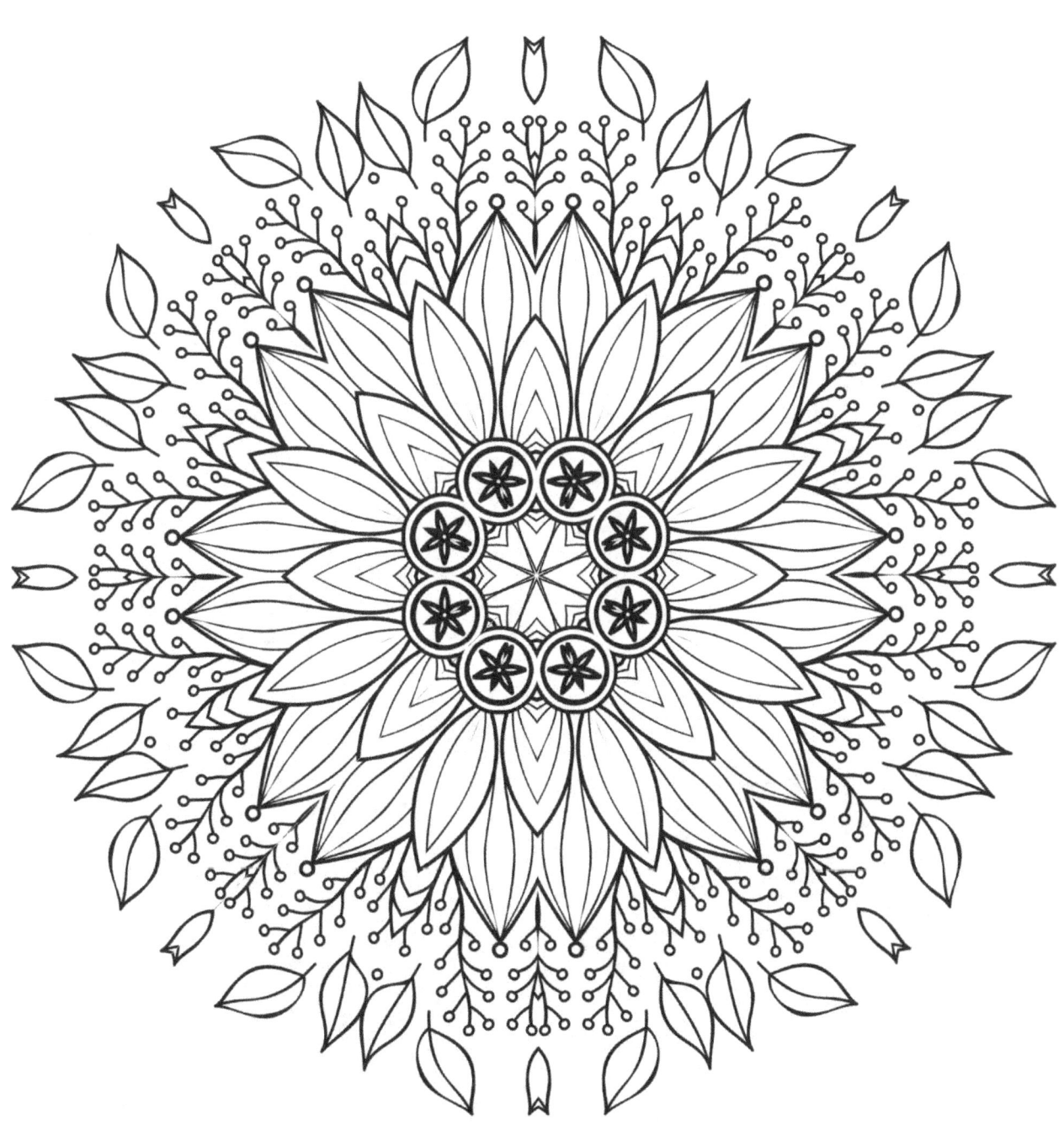

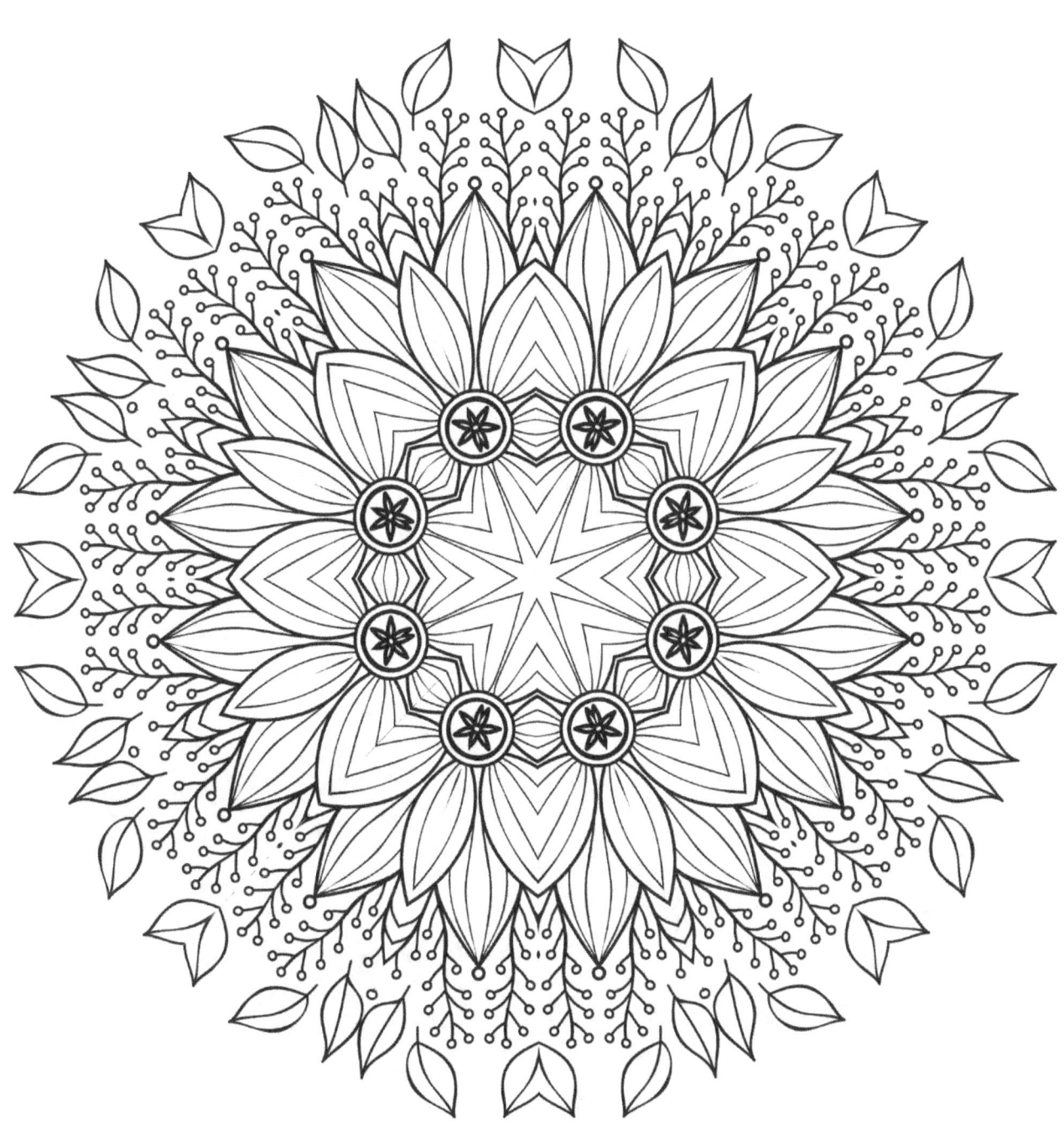

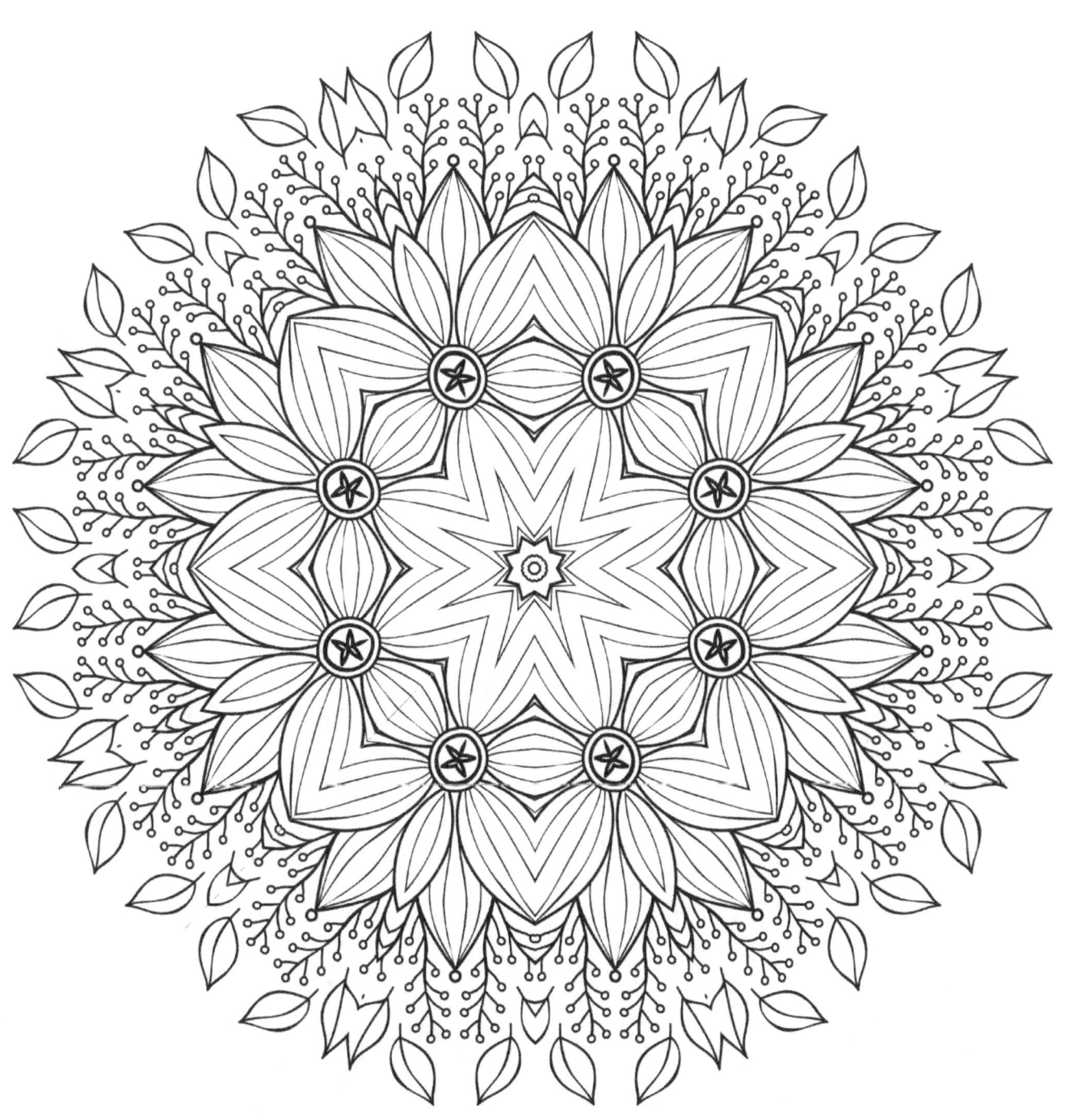

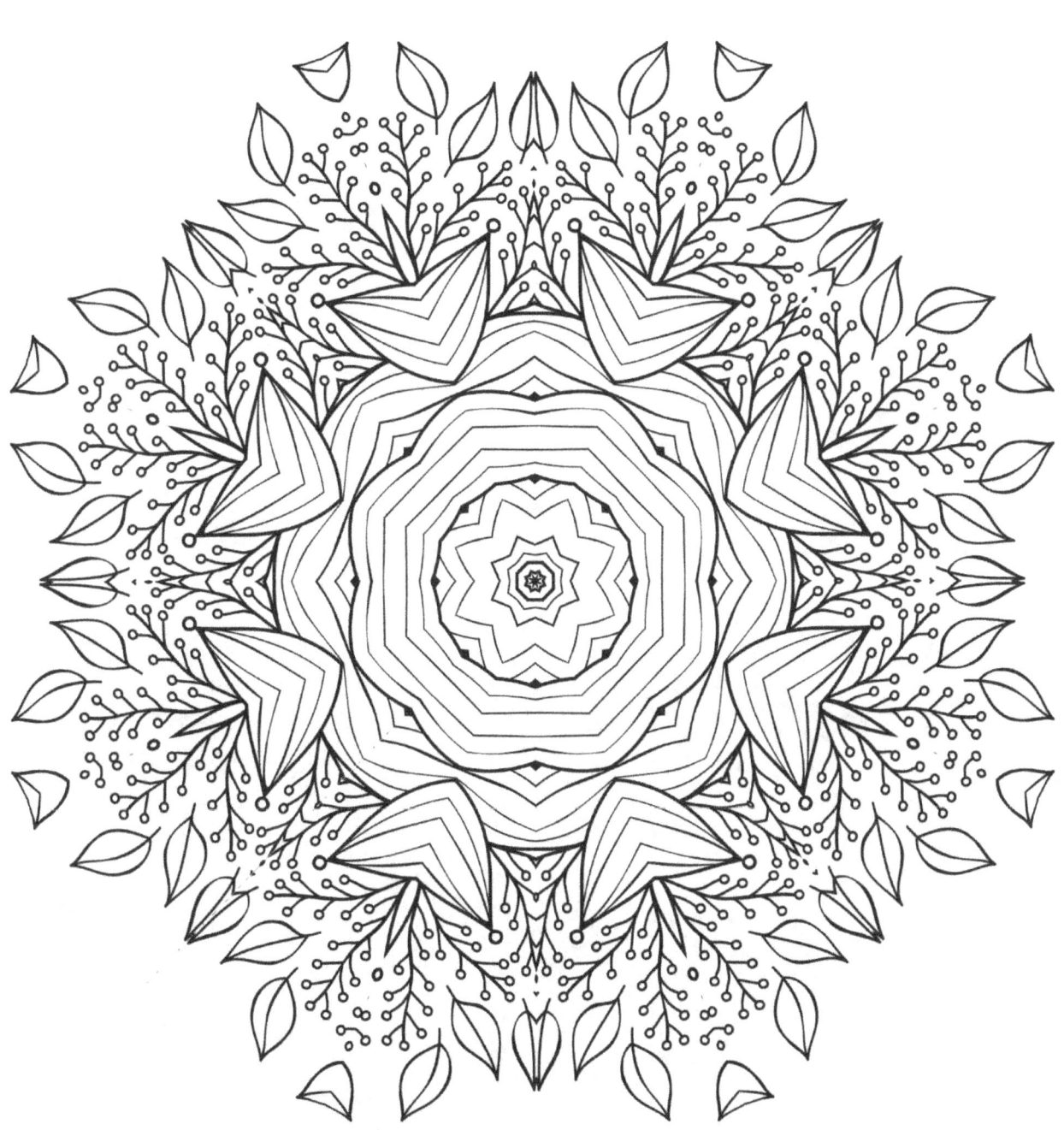

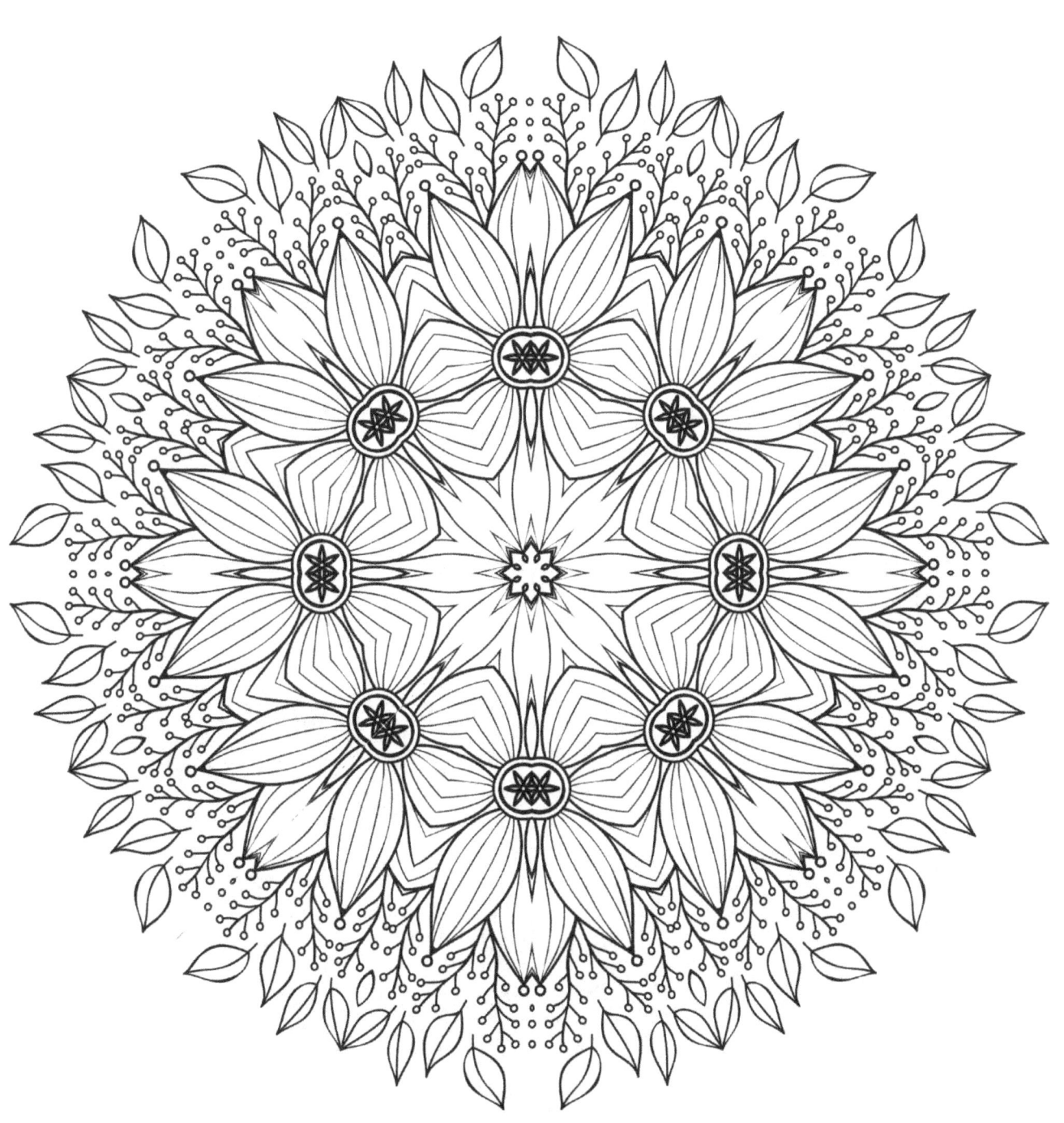

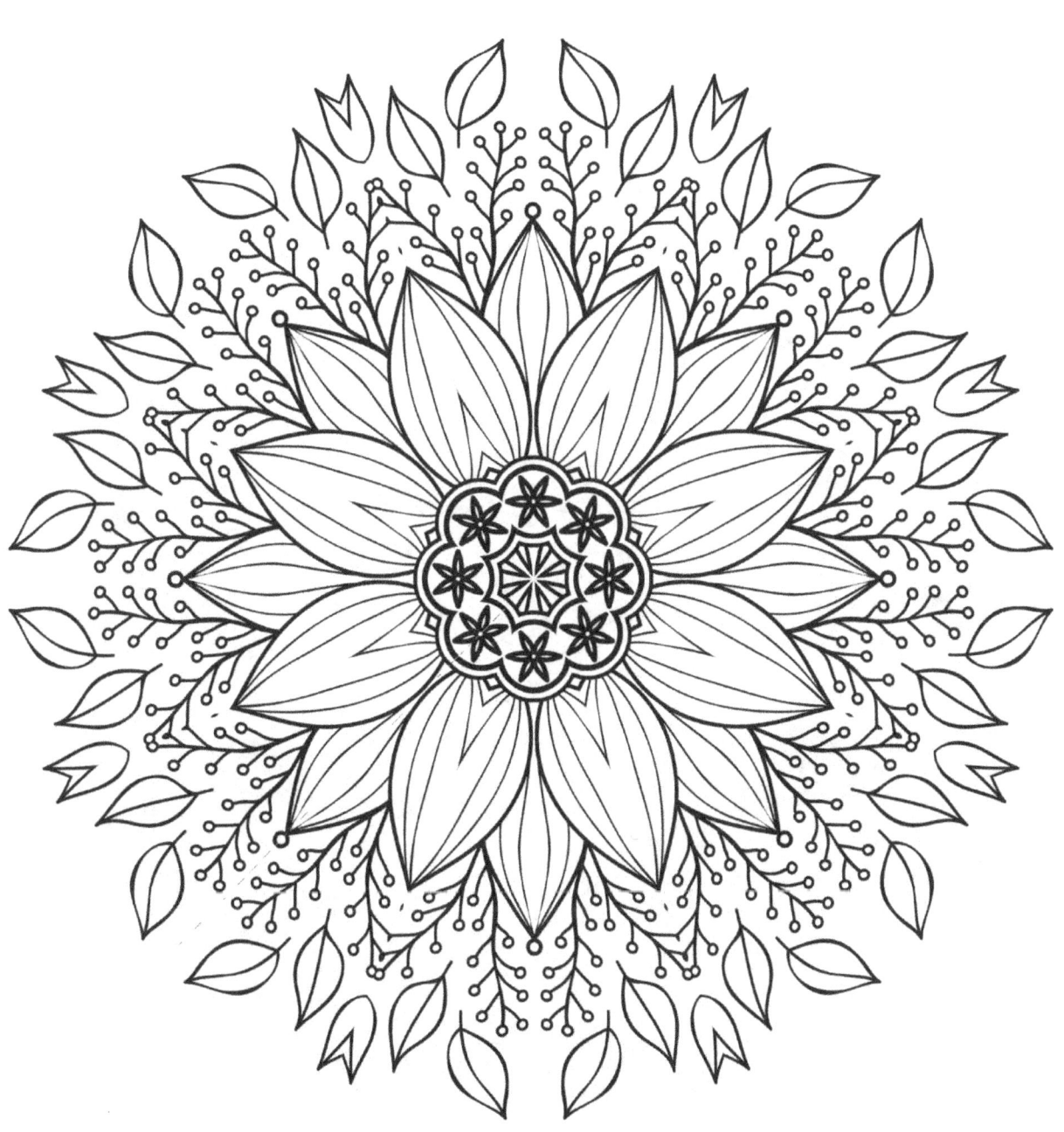

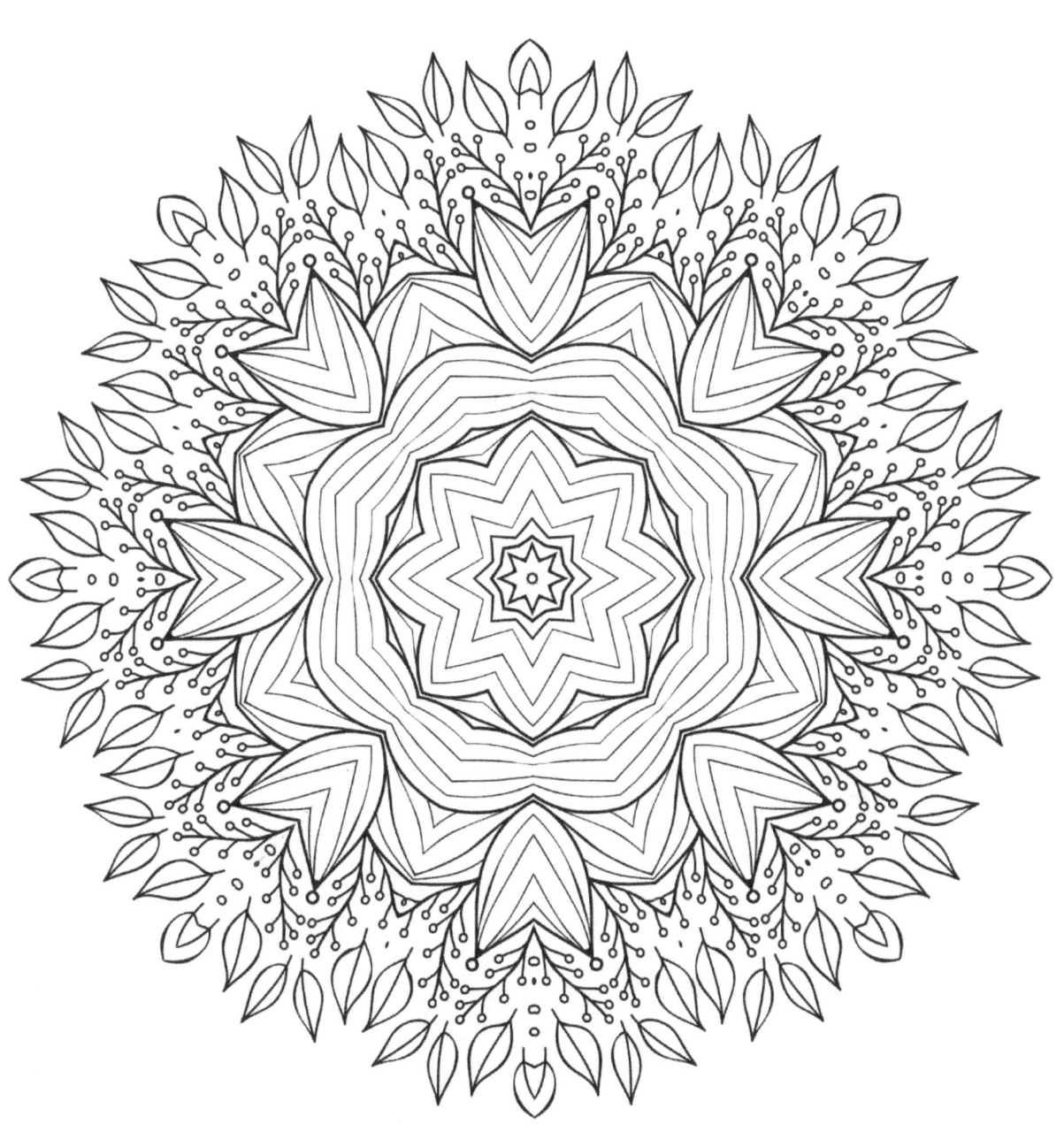

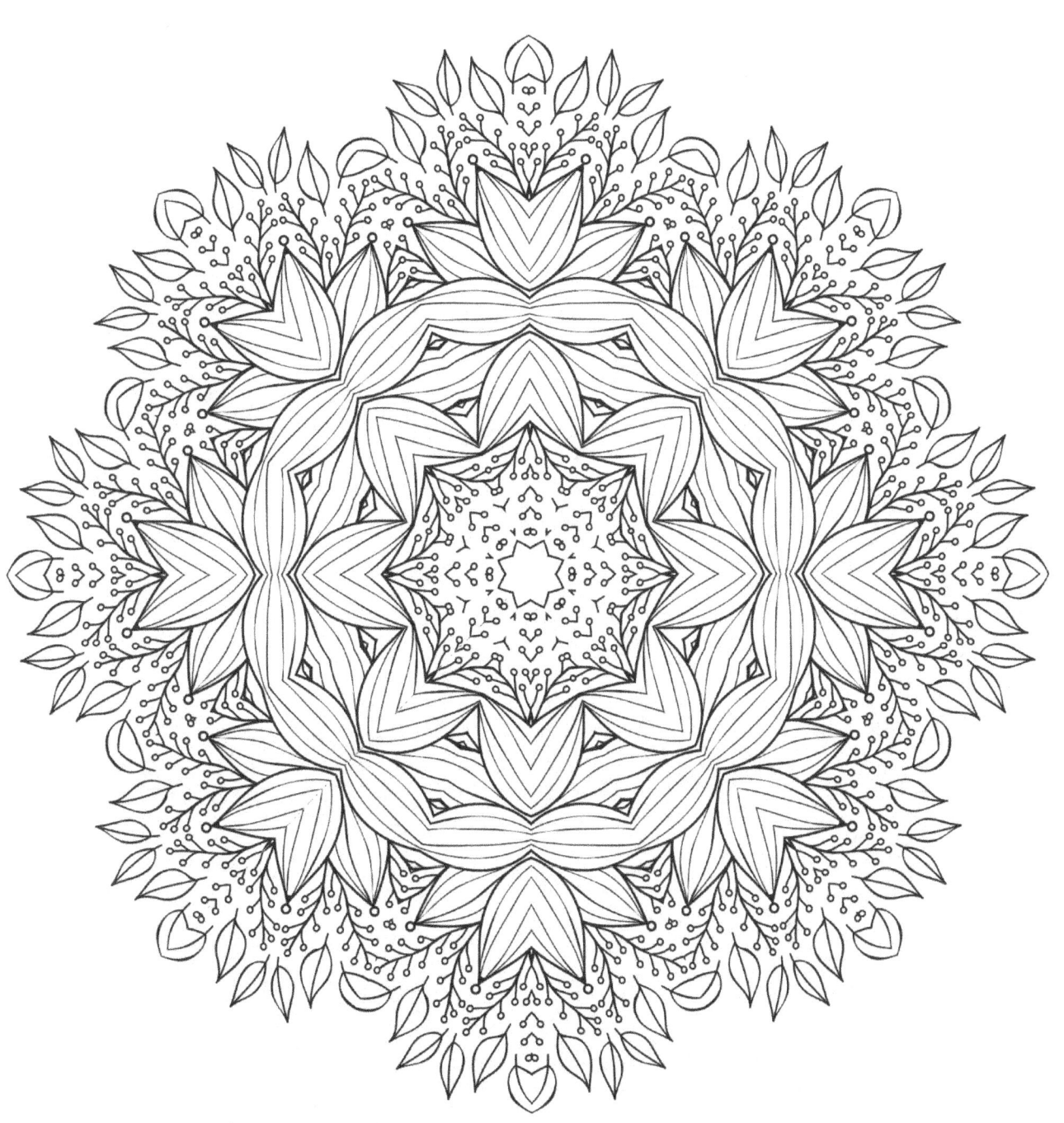

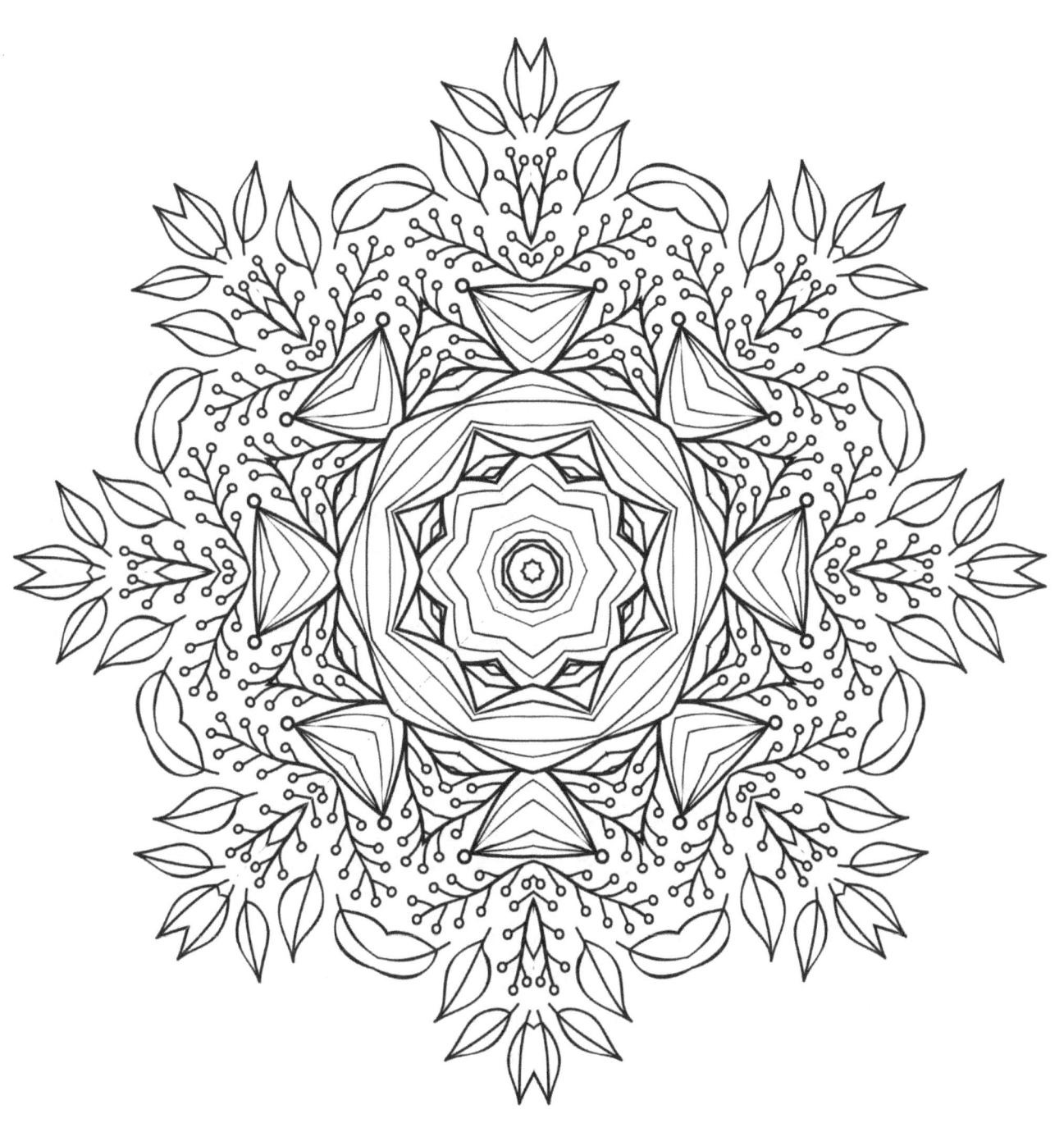

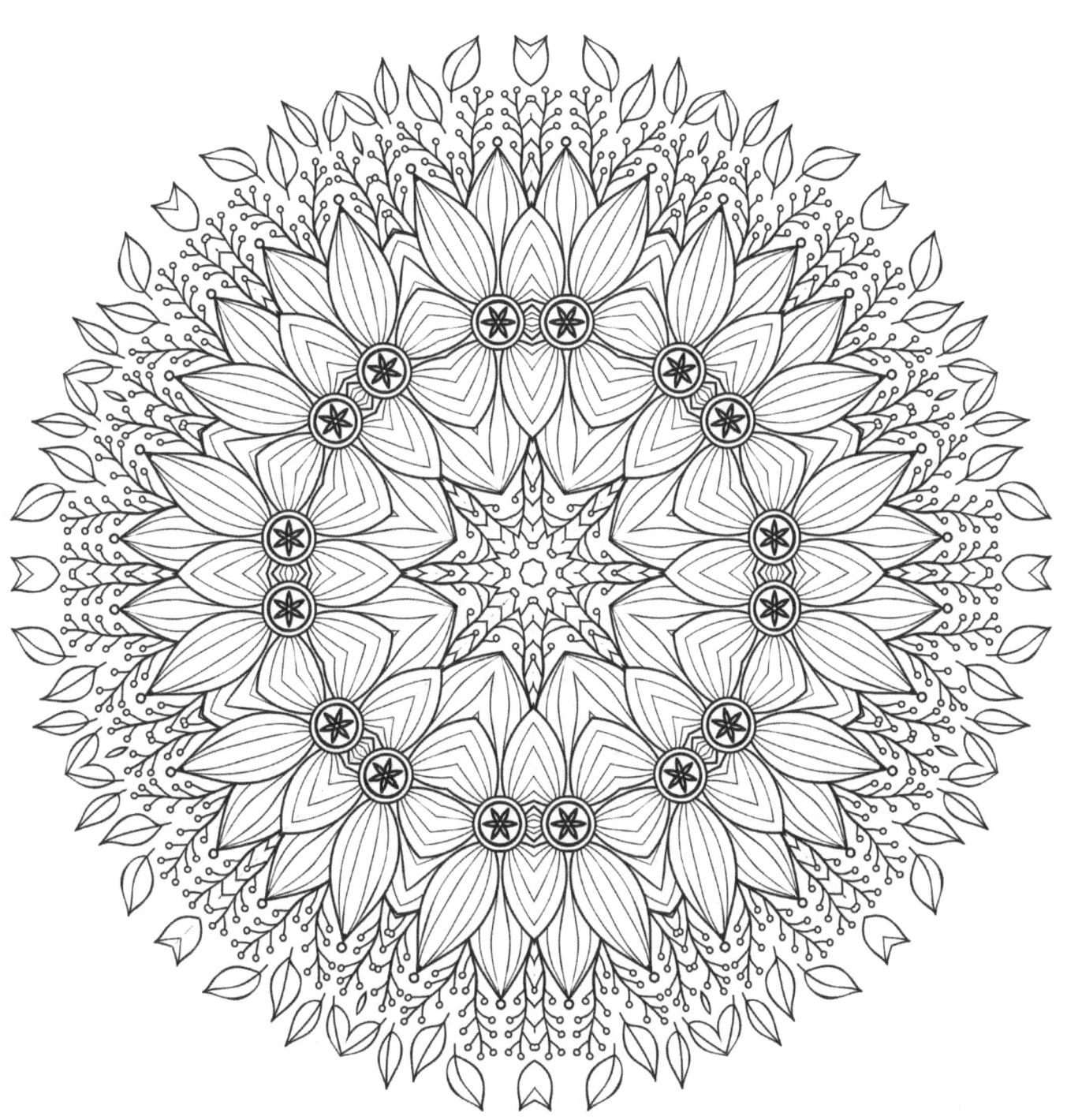

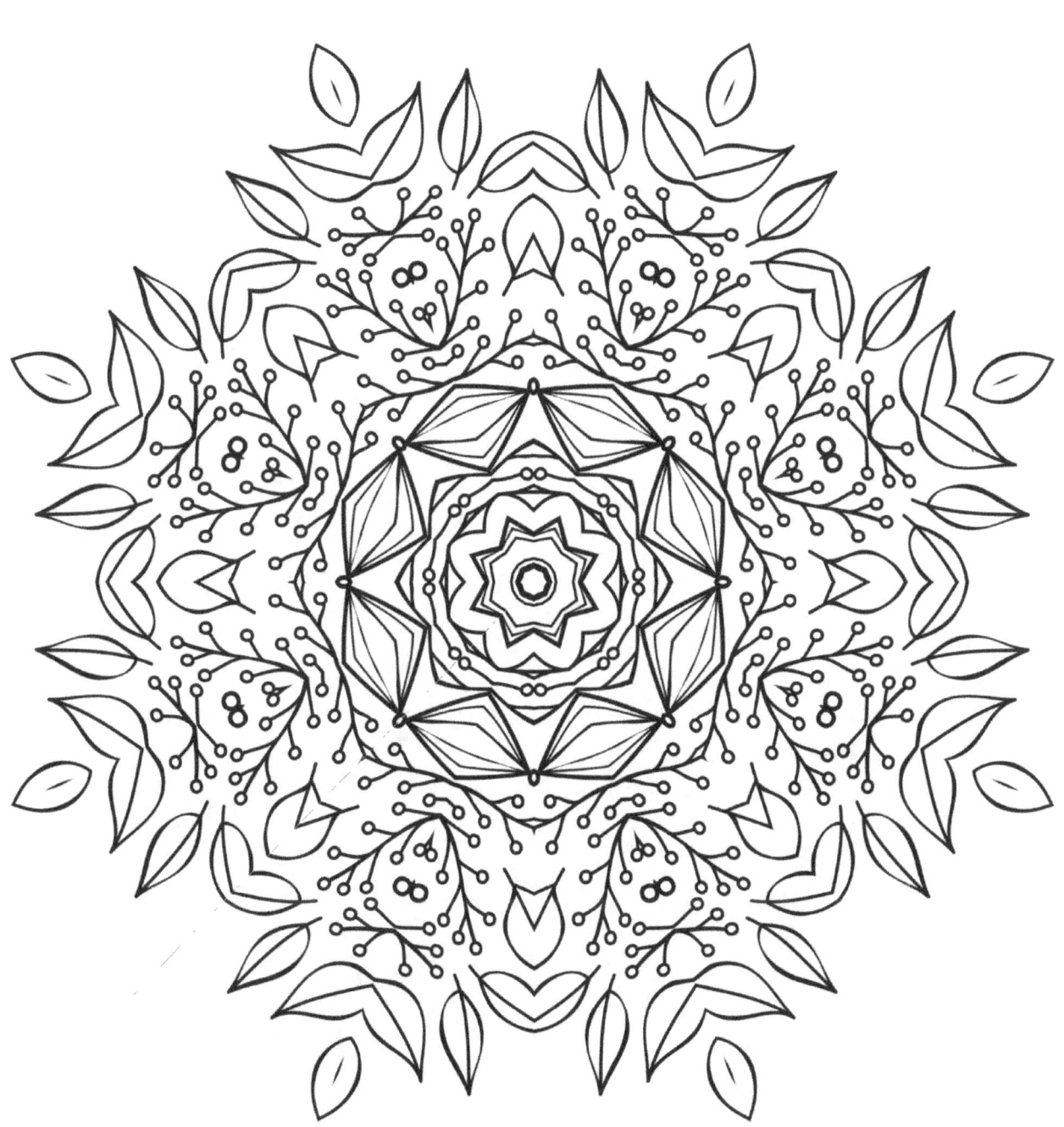

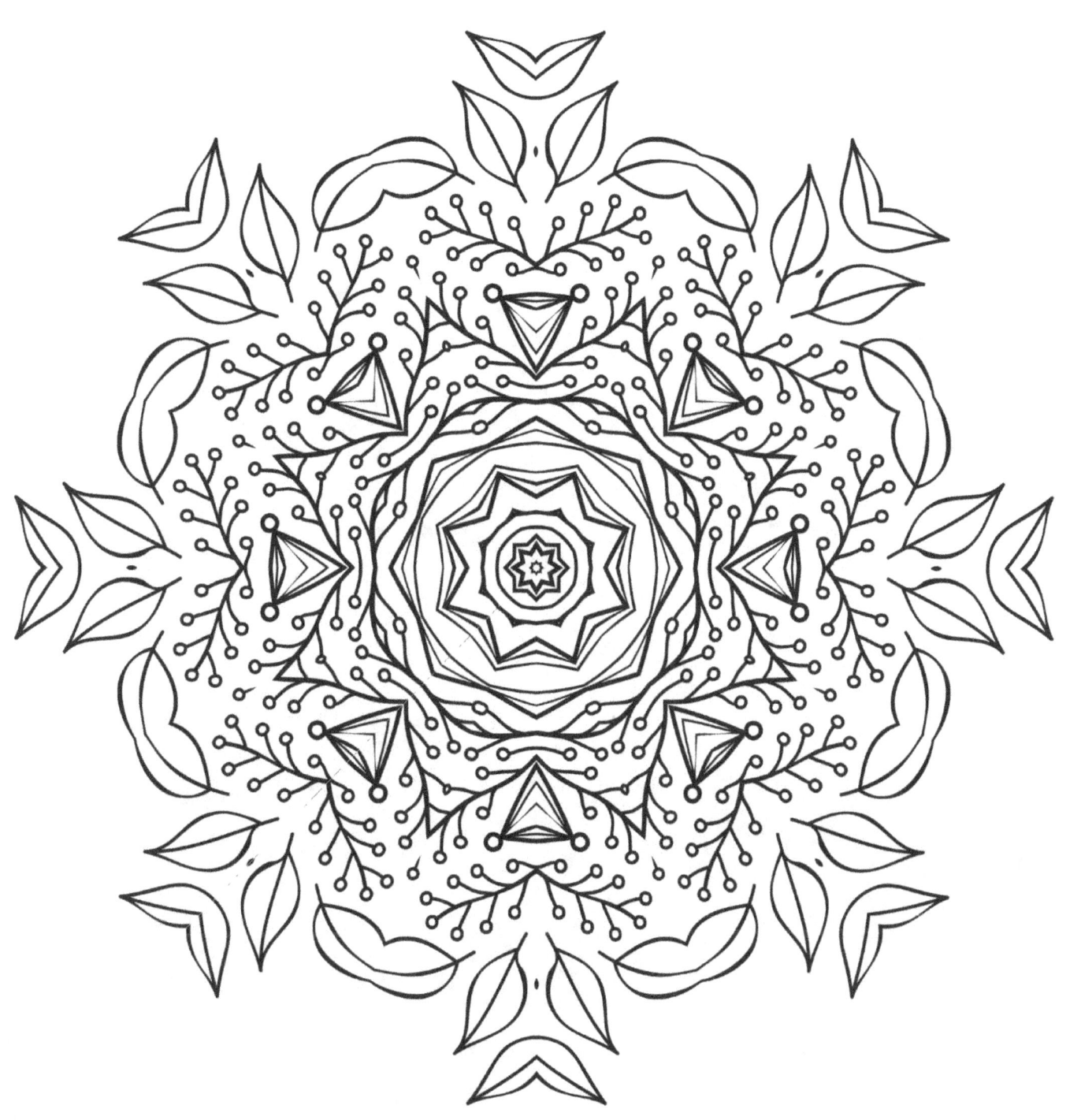

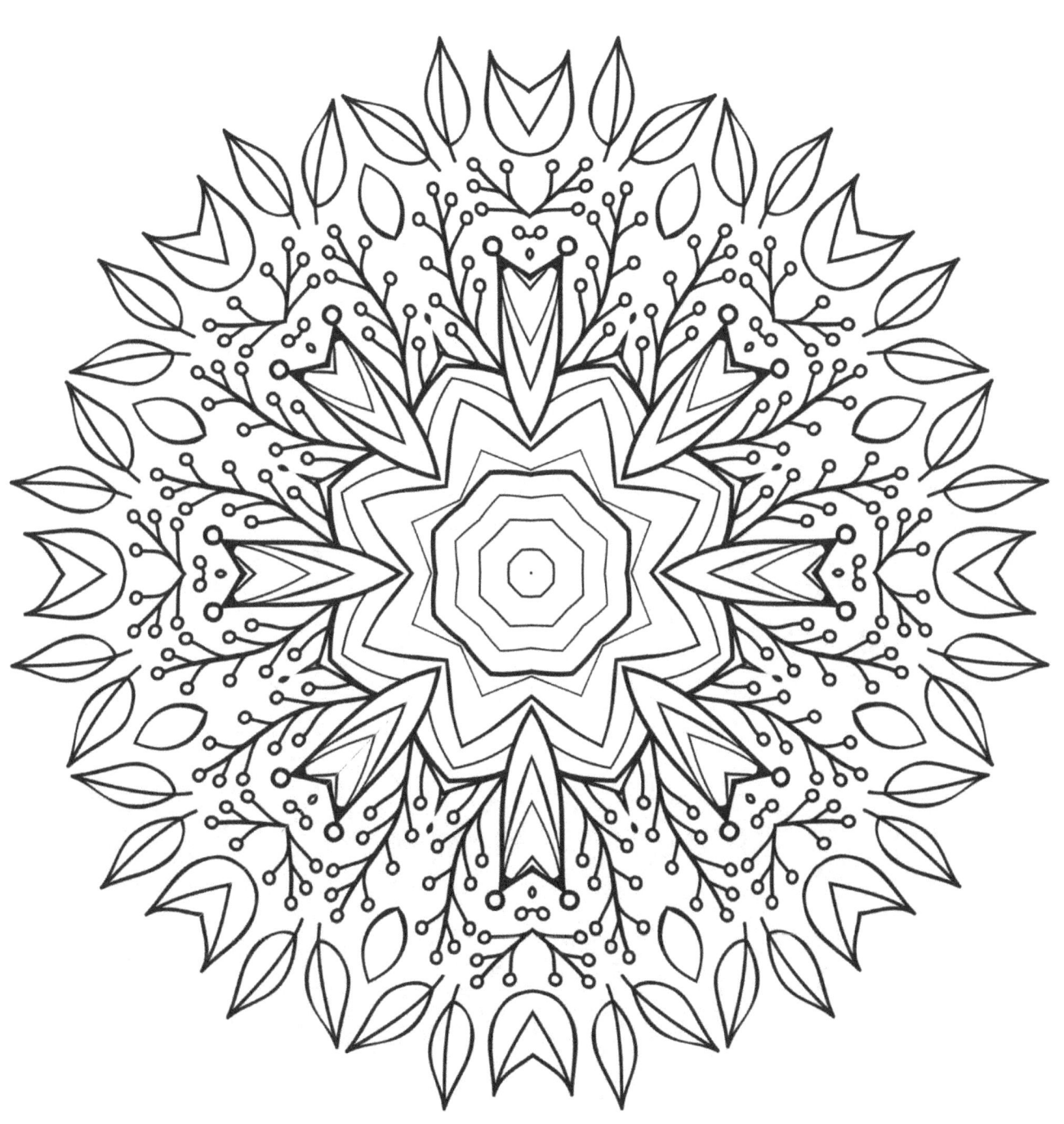

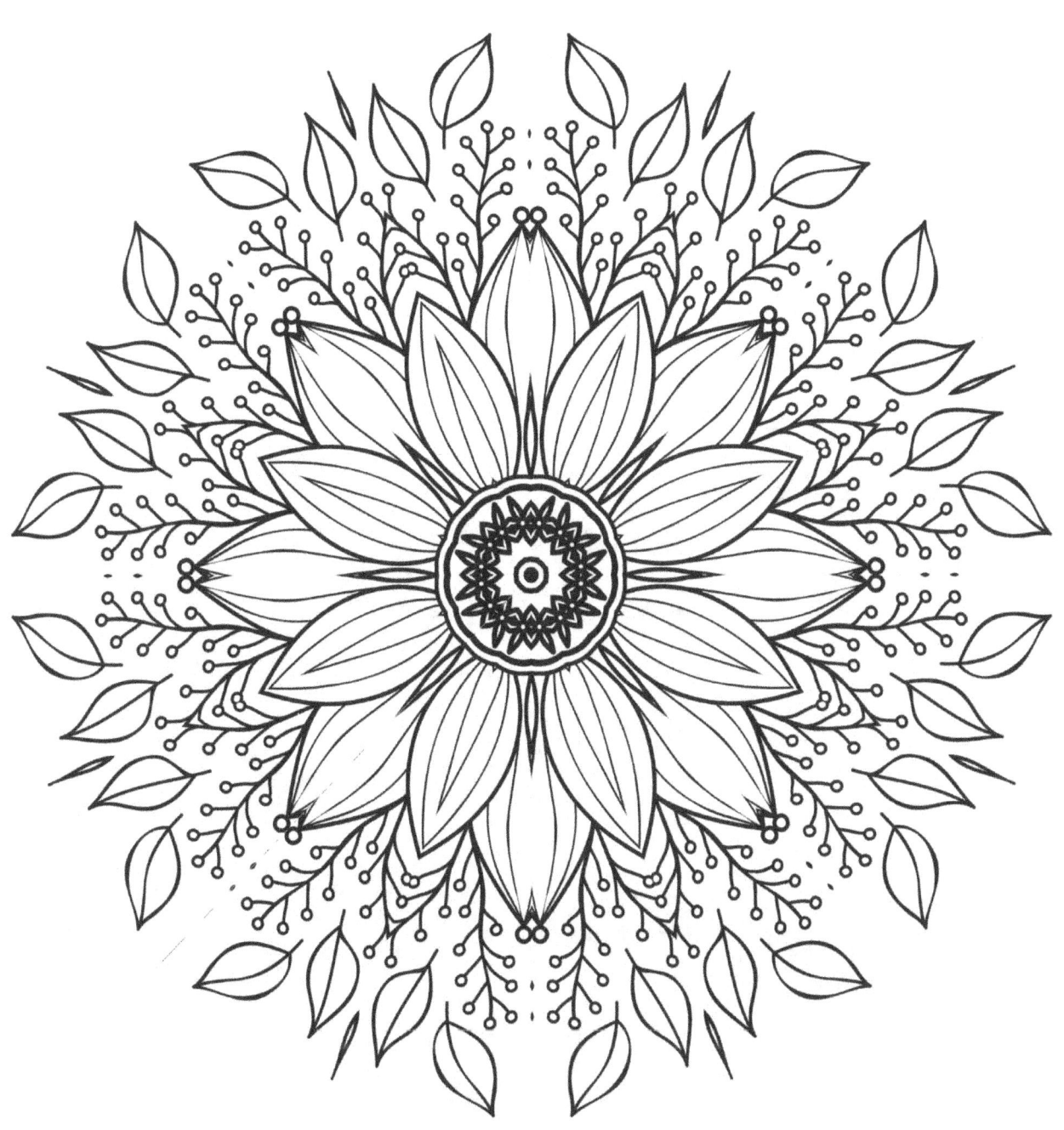

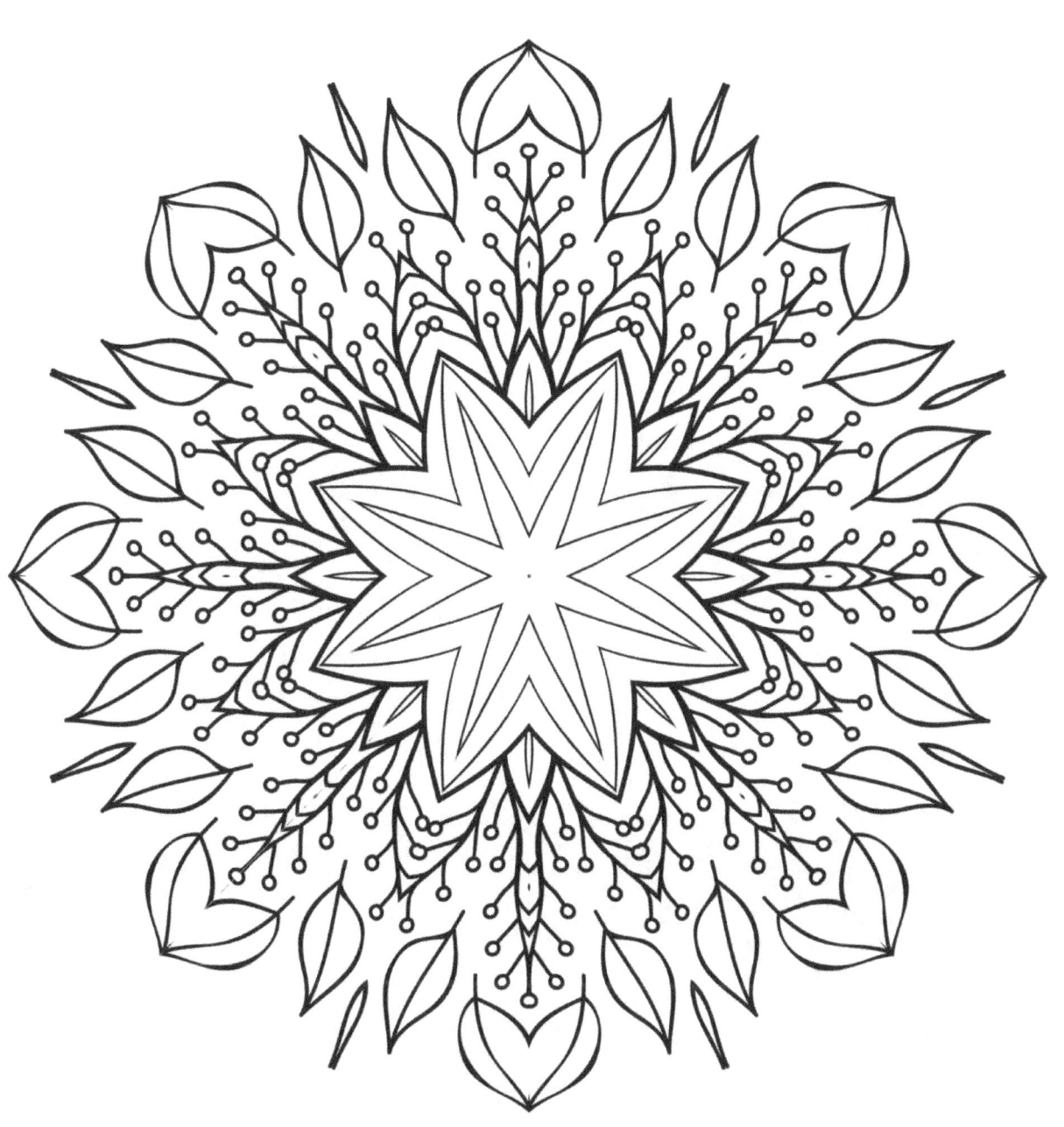

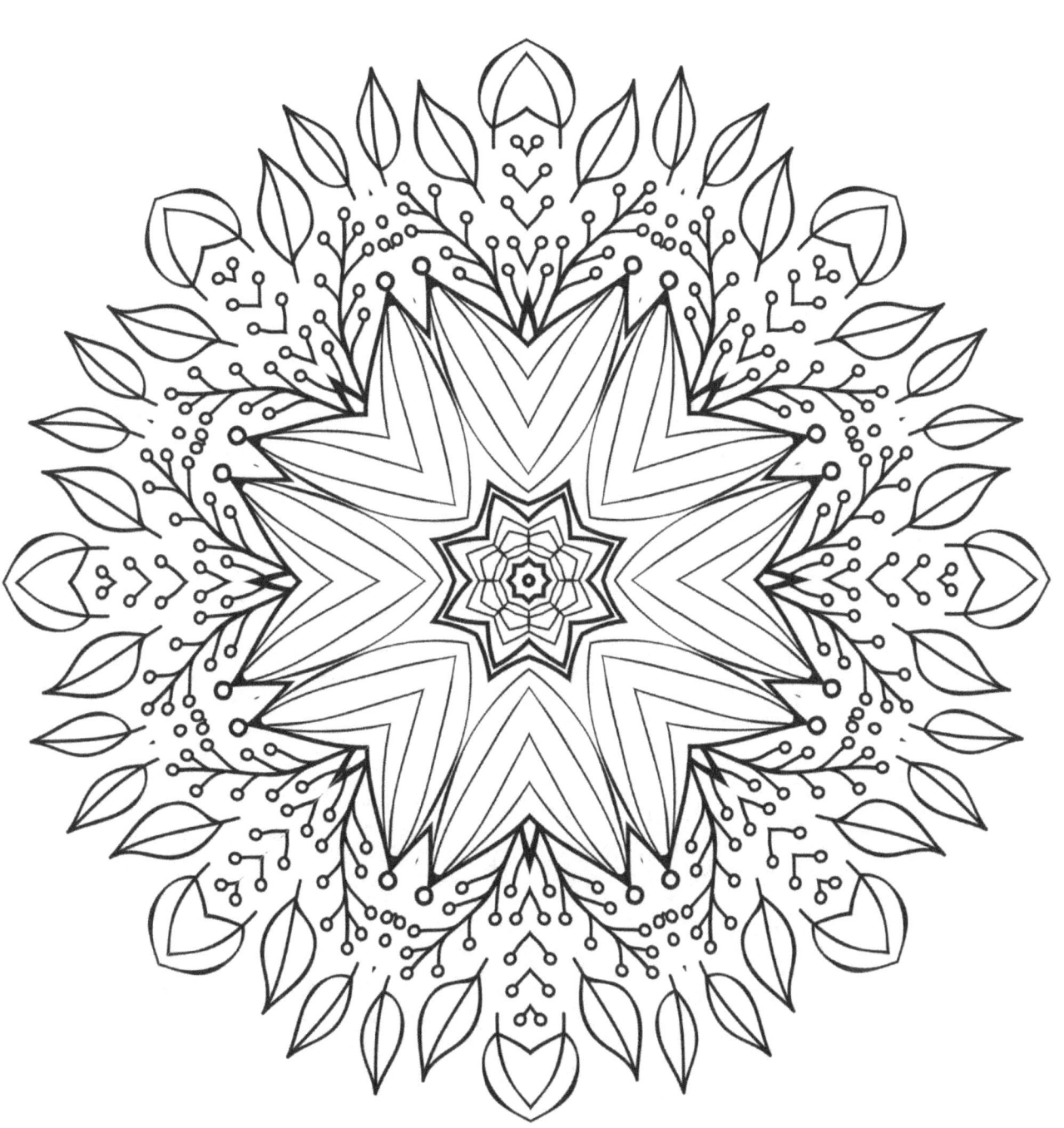

Hope you enjoy this coloring book.

Thank you.

www.ingramcontent.com/pod-product-compliance
Lightning Source LLC
Chambersburg PA
CBHW080835180526
45168CB00006B/2689